Nurturing Godly Children in an Ungodly World

Practical wisdom and faith-based strategies for today's parenting.

Romoking Onyebum

COPYRIGHT

Book Design by Anna Hannah

CONTENTS

DEDICATION

In loving memory of my biological parents, the late Mr. and Mrs. Clement and Victoria Onyebum,

Though you are no longer with us, your love, sacrifices, and unwavering belief in me continue to inspire every aspect of my life. This book is dedicated to your memory, with deepest gratitude for the foundation of faith and strength you provided. Your legacy lives on in the values you instilled in me. May this work honor your lives and encourage others to embrace faith and resilience in their own journeys.

With enduring love and gratitude.

ACKNOWLEDGEMENT

My deepest gratitude to Almighty God, whose love, grace, and mercy have been indispensable on this journey.

To my beloved wife, Nkeiruka Onyebum, your friendship and unwavering support have been my anchor. To my children Prince Onyebuchi, Princess Sochikaima, Cherish Amarachi, and Pearl Chimamanda you are my constant inspiration. Your faith, curiosity, and resilience motivate me every day. I love you dearly.

I am profoundly thankful to my foster parents, Mr. and Mrs. Osita Okpara, whose love and guidance have shaped my character.

And to my brother, Daniel Nwosu, CEO of CloudElite, your unwavering support has been invaluable, you are a brother indeed.

To my entire family, thank you for your love and encouragement throughout this journey.

INTRODUCTION

THE CHALLENGE OF RAISING GODLY CHILDREN TODAY

Dear Christian Parents and Adults,

In a world filled with temptation and moral decay, the task of raising godly children has never been more challenging. As parents, we are constantly bombarded with negative influences and distractions that threaten to lead our children astray. From social media to peer pressure, it can feel like an uphill battle to instill strong Christian values in our kids. However, we must remember that God has entrusted us with the precious responsibility of nurturing our children in His ways, and with His guidance, we can overcome any obstacle that comes our way.

As we navigate the complexities of raising children in an ungodly world, it is important to remember that we are not alone in this journey. God is always by our side, providing us with the strength and wisdom we need to lead our children on the right path. By seeking His guidance through prayer and studying His Word, we can equip ourselves with the tools necessary to navigate the challenges of modern parenting With God as our foundation, we can instill in our children a strong faith that will sustain them through the trials and temptations they may face.

One of the key challenges we face as parents is teaching our children to discern right from wrong in a world that often blurs the lines between morality and immorality. It is essential that we model godly behavior in our own lives, showing our children what it means to live a life of integrity and righteousness. By setting a positive example for our children to follow, we can help them develop a strong moral compass that will guide them in making wise choices as they navigate the complexities of the world around them.

In this book, "Nurturing Godly Children in an Ungodly World," we will explore practical strategies and biblical principles that can help us raise our children to be strong, faithful followers of Christ. Through stories, insights, and practical advice, we will learn how to cultivate a nurturing environment that fosters spiritual growth and moral development in our children. Together, we can rise to the challenge of raising godly children in an ungodly world, knowing that God is with us every step of the way.

Let us embark on this journey together with faith and de- termination, trusting in God's promises and relying on His grace to guide us in the noble task of Nurturing Godly Children in an Ungodly World. May we be encouraged and in- spired by the knowledge that we are not alone in this endeavor but are united in purpose and faith as we seek to raise a generation of children who will shine as lights in a dark and troubled world?

Raising children in today's world can feel like an uphill battle, especially when you're trying to instill strong Christian values. Everywhere you look, there seem to be influences that push against the principles we hold dear. From TV shows and music to what kids learn at school and see online, it's easy to feel overwhelmed and unsure about how to guide them. But take heart, dear parents, for you are not alone in this journey. God has equipped you with the wisdom and strength to navigate these challenges and lead your children toward a life rooted in faith.

It may seem like the world is constantly trying to pull your children away from their Christian beliefs but remember that God is always by your side, ready to guide you in raising your little ones in a way that honors Him. Each day presents a new opportunity to teach your children about the love and grace of God and to show them how to live out their faith in a world that may not always understand or accept it. Take comfort in the knowledge that you are planting seeds of faith that will grow and flourish in your children's hearts.

As Christian parents, it is important to be intentional in the way we raise our children. This means being mindful of the media they consume, the friends they spend time with, and the values they are exposed to on a daily basis. While it may be tempting to shield them from the world entirely, it is more beneficial to teach them how to navigate the challenges they will inevitably face while staying true to their Christian beliefs. By setting a positive example and providing them with a strong foundation in God's word, you are preparing them to stand firm in their faith no matter what the world throws their way.

Remember that you are not alone in this journey of raising godly children in an ungodly world. Lean on your faith, your community, and your church for support and guidance. Surround yourself and your children with positive influences that will help reinforce the values you hold dear. And most importantly, trust in God's plan for your family and have faith that He will lead you and your children on the path toward righteousness.

In the midst of all the challenges and temptations that come with raising children in today's world, remember to celebrate the victories, no matter how small they may seem. Every moment spent teaching your children about God's love, every prayer whispered for their protection, and every hug given in love is a step towards nurturing godly children in an ungodly world. Stay strong, stay faithful, and know that God is with you every step of the way.

This book is here to help. It's a practical guide for parents who want to raise their children with a strong, lasting faith. We'll cover the basics of Christian parenting, offer tips for handling everyday issues, and provide encouragement for those times when you feel lost or alone.

Welcome to "Nurturing Godly Children in an Ungodly World." This book is here to help you, dear Christian parents, navigate the challenges of raising children in today's world. We understand the importance of instilling a strong, lasting faith in your children, and we are here to provide you with practical guidance and support along the way.

In this subchapter, we will cover the basics of Christian parenting, offering you valuable insights and strategies to help you raise your children with a solid foundation in faith. From teaching them about the Bible to leading by example, we will explore the essential elements of nurturing godly children in an ungodly world.

We know that parenting is not always easy, and that's why we're here to offer you tips for handling everyday issues that may arise. Whether it's dealing with peer pressure, navigating social media, or addressing difficult questions about faith, we have the resources and advice you need to guide your children through these challenges with grace and wisdom.

And for those times when you feel lost or alone in your journey as a Christian parent, we want to offer you encouragement and support. Remember, you are not alone in this journey. With faith, perseverance, and the support of a com- munity of like-minded parents, you can raise your children to be strong, faithful, and resilient in the face of temptation.

So, take heart, dear parents. This book is your guide, your companion, and your source of inspiration as you navigate the rewarding yet challenging path of Nurturing Godly Children in an Ungodly World. Together, we can raise children who shine brightly as beacons of God's love and grace in an ungodly world.

One of the biggest challenges we face today is the sheer pace of life. It's easy to get caught up in the busyness and forget to be intentional about how we raise our children. But being a parent means more than just getting through the day. It means actively teaching and modeling the values and behaviors we want our children to learn. This book will help you create a home where faith is not just talked about but lived out every day.

In today's fast-paced world, it can be easy to get caught up in the hustle and bustle of life and forget to be intentional about how we raise our children. As Christian parents and adults, we face the challenge of balancing the demands of daily life with the responsibility of actively teaching and modeling the values and behaviors we want our children to learn. It's important to remember that being a parent is more than just getting through the day - it's about creating a home where faith is not just talked about but lived out every day.

In "Nurturing Godly Children in an Ungodly World," we aim to provide you with the tools and guidance you need to create a nurturing and faith-filled environment for your children. This book will help you navigate the challenges of raising children in an increasingly ungodly world and empower you to instill strong Christian values in your children. By being intentional about how you raise your children, you can make a lasting impact on their lives and help them grow into faithful followers of Christ.

As you read through the pages of this book, remember that you are not alone in your journey of nurturing godly children. There is a community of Christian parents and adults who face similar challenges and share a common goal of raising children who love and serve the Lord. Together, we can support and encourage one another as we strive to create homes where faith is lived out in every aspect of life.

It's important to approach the task of raising godly children with a spirit of encouragement and positivity. Instead of feeling overwhelmed by the pressures of modern life, focus on the unique opportunity you have to shape the hearts and minds of your children. By embracing this calling with joy and enthusiasm, you can create a home where faith is not just a Sunday morning activity but a way of life that permeates every moment.

In closing, remember that nurturing godly children is a journey that requires dedication, patience, and prayer. As you embark on this important task, know that you are making a difference in the lives of your children and in the world around you. With the help of this book and the support of your fellow Christian parents and adults, you can create a home where faith flourishes, and God's love shines brightly.

We'll also talk about the power of prayer. Prayer is more than just a routine; it's a way to connect with God and seek His guidance. We'll discuss how you can make prayer a natural part of your family's life and how to teach your children to pray, too.

In this subchapter, we will delve into the transformative power of prayer in nurturing godly children in a world filled with temptation. Prayer is not just a mere ritual or routine; it is a powerful tool that allows us to connect with God and seek His guidance in our lives. By incorporating prayer into your family's daily routine, you can create a strong foundation of faith that will help your children navigate the challenges of the world around them.

As Christian parents and adults, it is essential to make prayer a natural and integral part of your family's life. By setting an example of consistent prayer and communication with God, you can demonstrate to your children the importance of seeking God's guidance in all aspects of life. Encourage your children to pray with you, whether it be before meals, before bedtime, or during times of difficulty. By fostering a culture of prayer in your home, you are instilling in your children a deep and abiding faith that will serve them well throughout their lives.

Teaching your children to pray is a vital aspect of raising godly children in an ungodly world. By guiding them in how to communicate with God and express their thoughts, feelings, and needs through prayer, you are equipping them with a powerful tool for spiritual growth and resilience. Encourage your children to pray not only for themselves but also for others, fostering a spirit of compassion, empathy, and interconnectedness with the world around them.

Prayer is a profound and transformative practice that can strengthen your family's bond and faith in God. By incorporating prayer into your family's daily routine and teaching your children the importance of seeking God's guidance, you are nurturing godly children who are equipped to navigate the challenges of the world with grace and courage. Embrace the power of prayer in your family's life, and watch as God's guidance and blessings unfold in miraculous ways.

In conclusion, prayer is a powerful tool that can help you nurture godly children in a world filled with temptation. By making prayer a natural part of your family's life and teaching your children to pray, you are instilling in them a deep and abiding faith that will guide them through life's trials and tribulations. Embrace the power of prayer, and watch as God's grace and guidance transform your family into a beacon of light and hope in a world that desperately needs it.

In addition, we'll look at how to help your children navigate a world full of mixed messages. It's crucial to teach them to think critically about what they see and hear and to compare it against what the Bible says. We'll provide tips on how to have meaningful conversations with your children about their faith and help them understand and stand firm in biblical truth.

As Christian parents, it is our responsibility to guide our children through the maze of conflicting messages they en- counter on a daily basis. We must equip them with the tools they need to discern right from wrong, truth from falsehood. By encouraging them to think critically and compare everything they hear and see against the teachings of the Bible, we can help them develop a strong foundation of faith that will guide them through life's challenges.

One way to help your children navigate a world full of mixed messages is to engage them in open and honest conversations about their faith. Encourage them to ask questions, express their doubts, and share their struggles. By creating a safe and nurturing environment where they feel comfortable discussing their beliefs, you can help them develop a deeper understanding of God's word and how it applies to their lives.

It's important to remember that these conversations are not meant to be one sided lectures, but rather opportunities for mutual learning and growth. Listen to your children with an open heart and mind, and be willing to admit when you don't have all the answers. By engaging in meaningful dialogue with your children about their faith, you can help them develop a strong sense of self and a firm foundation in biblical truth.

By teaching your children to think critically, have meaningful conversations about their faith, and stand firm in biblical truth, you are equipping them with the tools they need to navigate a world full of mixed messages. As Christian parents, it is our duty to nurture our children in the ways of the Lord and help them grow into strong, faithful followers of Christ. With love, patience, and guidance, we can help our children navigate the challenges of an ungodly world and stand firm in their beliefs.

Raising godly children is not easy, but it's incredibly rewarding. There's nothing more fulfilling than seeing your children grow into loving, faithful, and compassionate people. This book is here to walk with you on this journey, offering practical advice and encouragement along the way. Together, let's embark on the mission of nurturing godly children in an ungodly world, trusting that with God's help, we can make a lasting impact on their lives.

As Christian parents and adults, we are faced with the daunting task of raising our children in a world filled with temptation and distraction. It can be overwhelming at times, but remember that you are not alone in this journey. God is with you every step of the way, guiding you and providing you with the strength and wisdom you need to raise your children according to His will.

One of the key aspects of nurturing godly children is leading by example. Our children learn from watching us, so it's important to model the values and behaviors we want to instill in them. Show them what it means to have a strong faith, to be kind and compassionate, and to stand firm in the face of temptation. Your actions speak louder than words, so let your light shine brightly for your children to see.

In a world that often promotes selfishness, materialism, and instant gratification, it's crucial that we teach our children the importance of faith, humility, and service to others.

Encourage them to cultivate a personal relationship with God through prayer, scripture reading, and participation in church activities. Help them develop a heart for serving others and show them the joy that comes from living a life of purpose and meaning.

Remember, the journey of raising godly children is a marathon, not a sprint. It takes time, patience, and perseverance to mold your children into the individuals God has called them to be. Trust in God's plan for your family, lean on Him for strength and guidance, and never underestimate the power of prayer. With God's help, you can make a lasting impact on your children's lives and raise them to be beacons of light in a dark and ungodly world.

CHAPTER ONE

UNDERSTANDING THE UNGODLY WORLD

*a*s Christian parents and adults, we are faced with the daunting task of nurturing godly children in a world filled with temptation. It can often feel overwhelming to navigate through the ungodly influences that surround our children on a daily basis. However, it is crucial for us to first understand the nature of this ungodly world in order to effectively guide our children towards godliness.

One of the key aspects of understanding the ungodly world is recognizing the pervasive presence of sin and temptation in our society. From the media to peer pressure, our children are constantly bombarded with messages that go against the teachings of the Bible. It is important for us to equip our children with the knowledge

1

and discernment to recognize these temptations and respond in a godly manner.

Furthermore, we must also acknowledge the role of spiritual warfare in the ungodly world. The enemy is constantly seeking to lead our children astray and we must be vigilant in protecting them from his schemes. By teaching our children to put on the full armor of God and rely on the power of prayer, we can help them resist the attacks of the enemy and stand firm in their faith.

In addition, it is essential for us to cultivate a strong foundation of faith within our children. By instilling in them a deep love for God and His Word, we can help them develop a firm belief in the truth of the Gospel. This foundation will not only guide them in making godly decisions, but also provide them with the strength and courage to resist the temptations of the ungodly world.

Overall, while the ungodly world may seem daunting, we must remember that we serve a God who is greater than any temptation or evil influence. By understanding the nature of the ungodly world and equipping our children with the tools to navigate through it, we can raise up a generation of godly children who will shine brightly in the darkness. Let us take heart and trust in the Lord as we embark on this journey of Nurturing Godly Children in an Ungodly World.

To help your children grow up with strong faith, it's important to understand the world they live in. Today's world is very different from what it used to be. There are many things around them that can pull them away from their faith. In this chapter, we'll look at these things and how they can affect your children.

As Christian parents and adults, it is our responsibility to guide our children and help them navigate through the challenges of the world. We must be aware of the temptations and distractions that can lead them astray from their faith. By understanding the world they live in, we can better equip ourselves to protect and nurture their Godly upbringing.

One of the biggest challenges our children face today is the constant exposure to technology and social media. These platforms can bombard them with messages that contradict their Christian values. It's important for us to monitor their screen time and teach them how to use technology responsibly. By setting boundaries and having open conversations about what they see online, we can help them discern what is in line with their faith and what is not.

Another factor that can influence our children's faith is peer pressure. As they grow older, they may encounter friends who have different beliefs or engage in behaviors that go against their Christian values. It's crucial for us to instill in them a strong foundation of faith so that they can confidently stand firm in their beliefs, even in the face of peer pressure.

In this chapter, we will explore practical ways to help your children grow up with strong faith in a world full of temptation. By being proactive and intentional in nurturing their Godly upbringing, we can empower them to live out their faith boldly and confidently. Let's work together to raise a generation of Godly children who will shine brightly in an ungodly world.

The Influence of Media and Technology

In today's world, the influence of media and technology on our children cannot be ignored. As Christian parents, it is our responsibility to be aware of the impact these external forces can have on our children's beliefs and values. While technology can be a useful tool for learning and communication, it can also be a dangerous gateway to harmful content and negative influences. It is crucial that we guide our children in using technology responsibly and help them navigate the digital world with wisdom and discernment.

One way we can counteract the negative influence of media and technology is by modeling positive behavior ourselves. Our children learn by example, so it is important for us to demonstrate healthy media consumption habits and prioritize face to face interactions over screen time. By setting boundaries and creating a media-free environment during family meals or bonding activities, we show our children the value of real life connections and meaningful conversations.

As Christian parents, we must also be vigilant in monitoring the content our children are exposed to. From television shows and movies to social media and video games, there is a constant barrage of messages that can shape our children's worldview. By actively engaging in discussions about the media our children consume and helping them discern between what is true and what is harmful, we can equip them with the tools they need to resist negative influences and stand firm in their faith.

It is also important for us to provide our children with alternative forms of entertainment and enrichment that align with our Christian values. Encouraging them to read books that promote virtues such as kindness, honesty, and compassion, or engaging in activities that foster creativity and critical thinking, can help counterbalance the negative messages they may encounter in the media. By creating a positive and nurturing environment at home, we can help our children develop a strong moral compass and resist the temptations of the world.

Ultimately, as Christian parents, our goal is to raise children who are grounded in their faith and equipped to navigate the challenges of a secular world. By being intentional in our approach to media and technology, we can help our children grow into godly individuals who are able to discern right from wrong and stand firm in their beliefs. Let us embrace this challenge with courage and faith, knowing that God is with us every step of the way as we nurture our children in a world filled with temptation.

Many of the things kids see on TV, the internet, and in video games can go against what the Bible teaches. It's important to keep an eye on what they're watching and playing.

Social Media: Platforms like Instagram and TikTok can make kids feel bad about themselves and desire things they don't need.

In today's digital age, social media has become a pervasive force in the lives of our children. Platforms like Instagram and TikTok can be both entertaining and informative, but they also have the potential to negatively impact our children's self-esteem and desires. As Christian parents, it is our responsibility to guide our children in navigating these platforms with wisdom and discernment.

It is important to recognize that social media often portrays a distorted version of reality. Many users on platforms like Instagram and TikTok carefully curate their content to show- case only the highlights of their lives, creating an unrealistic standard of beauty, success, and happiness. This can lead our children to compare themselves to others and feel inadequate or dissatisfied with their own lives.

Furthermore, the constant exposure to materialism and consumerism on social media can fuel our children's desires for things they don't truly need. The pressure to keep up with the latest trends and have the newest gadgets can breed dis- contentment and a sense of greed. As Christian parents, we must instill in our children the values of gratitude, contentment, and stewardship, reminding them that true happiness does not come from material possessions.

It is essential that we engage in open and honest conversations with our children about the potential pitfalls of social media. Encourage them to critically evaluate the content they consume and consider how it aligns with their values and beliefs as followers of Christ.

Help them cultivate a healthy sense of self-worth that is rooted in their identity as beloved children of God, rather than in the likes and comments they receive online.

Ultimately, as Christian parents, our goal is to nurture godly children who are able to navigate the temptations of this world with grace and wisdom. By setting a positive example with our own social media usage and providing guidance and support to our children, we can help them develop a healthy relationship with technology and social media that honors God and promotes their spiritual growth. Let us trust in the Lord to guide us in raising our children in a world filled with temptation, knowing that He is faithful to provide us with the strength and wisdom we need.

Television and Movies: Some shows and movies portray lifestyles and actions that don't align with biblical teachings.

Television and movies have become a common form of entertainment in today's society, but as Christian parents and adults, it is important to be mindful of the content that is being consumed by our children. Some shows and movies portray lifestyles and actions that don't align with biblical teachings, and it is our responsibility to guide our children in discerning right from wrong.

It can be challenging to navigate the vast array of media options available to us, but by being intentional about the shows and movies we allow our children to watch, we can help them develop a strong moral compass. Encouraging our children to think critically about the messages being portrayed on screen can empower them to make wise choices in their own lives.

As we strive to nurture godly children in an ungodly world, it is important to remember that we are called to be in the world but not of the world. This means being vigilant about the influences that shape our children's worldview and being proactive in providing them with alternative forms of entertainment that align with biblical values.

When discussing the potential harm that certain shows and movies can have on our children, it is important to approach the topic with love and understanding. Rather than banning certain content outright, we can use these opportunities to engage in meaningful conversations with our children about the importance of living according to God's word and the consequences of straying from His path.

By being intentional about the media our children consume and actively engaging them in conversations about biblical teachings, we can help them grow into strong, God-fearing individuals who are equipped to navigate the challenges of the world around them. Let us continue to nurture our children in the ways of the Lord, guiding them with love, patience, and grace as they navigate the complexities of today's media landscape.

Video Games: Certain games can normalize violence or distract kids from other important activities.

In today's digital age, video games have become a popular form of entertainment for children and teens. While some games can be harmless and even educational, it is important for Christian parents to be aware of the potential dangers that certain games can pose. As responsible adults, we must be vigilant in monitoring the content our children are exposed to, especially when it comes to violence in video games.

It is well-documented that certain video games can normalize violence and desensitize children to its effects. Studies have shown that exposure to violent video games can increase aggressive thoughts, feelings, and behaviors in children. As parents, it is our duty to protect our children from harmful influences and to instill in them the values of compassion, empathy, and non-violence.

Furthermore, excessive time spent playing video games can distract children from other important activities such as homework, physical exercise, and social interactions. As Christians, we are called to be good stewards of our time and resources, and it is crucial that we guide our children in making wise choices when it comes to how they spend their leisure time. Encouraging them to engage in a variety of activities that nurture their minds, bodies, and spirits is essential for their holistic development.

By setting limits on screen time and monitoring the content of the games our children play, we can help ensure that they are not being negatively influenced by violent or inappropriate material. It is also important to have open and honest conversations with our children about the impact of video games on their behavior and attitudes. By fostering a culture of communication and trust within our families, we can guide our children towards making wise choices and developing into godly individuals.

In conclusion, while video games can be a fun and engaging form of entertainment, it is crucial for Christian parents to be mindful of the potential risks they pose. By being pro- active in monitoring the content our children are exposed to and encouraging them to engage in a variety of activities that promote their overall wellbeing, we can help nurture them into godly individuals who are equipped to navigate the challenges of an ungodly world. Let us continue to pray for wisdom and discernment as we guide our children on the path of righteousness.

Secular Education and Peer Pressure

In today's society, secular education plays a significant role in shaping the minds and beliefs of our children. As Christian parents and adults, it is important to

11

recognize the impact that secular education can have on our children and be proactive in guiding them to stay true to their Christian values. While it is essential for our children to receive a quality education, it is equally important for us to instill in them a strong foundation in their faith.

One of the challenges that our children may face in a secular educational environment is peer pressure. It can be difficult for them to stand firm in their beliefs when they are surrounded by classmates who may not share the same values. As parents and adults, we must equip our children with the tools they need to resist negative peer pressure and stay true to their Christian principles. Encouraging open communication with our children and fostering a strong support system within our Christian community can help them navigate these challenges successfully.

It is crucial for us to be actively involved in our children's education and to reinforce the values and teachings of our faith at home. By engaging in discussions about what they are learning in school and providing guidance on how to apply their Christian beliefs to everyday situations, we can help them develop a strong sense of identity and purpose in a secular world. Encouraging our children to seek out positive influences and friendships that align with their values can also help them resist negative peer pressure and stay on the right path.

As Christian parents and adults, we must lead by example and demonstrate to our children the importance of living out our faith in all aspects of our lives. By showing them how to navigate the challenges of secular education with grace and integrity, we can empower them to do the same. Let us continue to nurture our children in the ways of the Lord, instilling in them a deep-rooted faith that will guide them through the trials and temptations of this ungodly world. Together, we can raise up a generation of godly children who will shine brightly in a world that desperately needs the light of Christ.

Schools sometimes teach things that don't align with biblical teachings, and friends can have a significant influence on kids, sometimes leading them astray.

School Lessons: Subjects like evolution may conflict with biblical views.

As Christian parents, it is important for us to be aware of the potential conflicts that may arise between our faith and what our children are learning in school. One such area of contention is the subject of evolution, which may conflict with biblical views of creation. It is natural to feel concerned about how our children will navigate these conflicting perspectives, but it is also an opportunity for us to engage in meaningful discussions with them about how to reconcile their faith with what they are learning in the classroom.

When our children are exposed to teachings that may contradict our beliefs, it is important for us to approach the situation with an open mind and a spirit of understanding. We can use these moments as opportunities to teach our children critical thinking skills and to help them develop a strong foundation of faith that can withstand challenges from the world around them. By engaging in conversations with our children about evolution and other potentially conflicting subjects, we can help them see that it is possible to hold different perspectives while still remaining true to their Christian beliefs. It is also important for us to remember that our children are individuals with their own thoughts and beliefs. While we may want to guide them in their faith journey, it is essential to allow them the space to ask questions and form their own opinions. By fostering an environment of open communication and respect, we can help our children develop a strong sense of self and a deep understanding of their faith.

As we navigate the challenges of raising godly children in an ungodly world, it is crucial to remember that our ultimate goal is to nurture them in their faith and help them grow into strong, resilient Christians. By approaching subjects like evolution with a spirit of encouragement and understanding, we can guide our children in developing a faith that is grounded in love, truth, and grace. Let us embrace these opportunities for growth and learning, trusting that God will guide us and our children on this journey of faith.

Friends: Kids often want to fit in, even if it means compromising their values.

In today's society, children are constantly bombarded with pressures to fit in with their peers. As Christian parents, it is important for us to teach our children the value of staying true to their beliefs and not compromising their values just to be accepted by others.

Friends play a significant role in a child's life, and it is crucial for us to guide our children in choosing friends who will up- lift and encourage them in their faith.

It is natural for kids to want to fit in and be accepted by their peers. However, as Christian parents, we must remind our children that their worth and identity come from God, not from the approval of others. Encourage your children to surround themselves with friends who share their values and beliefs, and who will support them in their walk with God. Remind them that true friends will love and accept them for who they are, without expecting them to compromise their faith.

As our children navigate the challenges of peer pressure, it is important for us to equip them with the tools they need to stand firm in their faith. Encourage open communication with your children, so they feel comfortable coming to you with any concerns or struggles they may have. Help them understand that it is okay to say no to things that go against their beliefs, and that true friends will respect their decisions.

As Christian parents, we must lead by example in our own relationships and friendships. Show your children what it looks like to have healthy, God honoring friendships by surrounding yourself with like-minded individuals who will encourage and support you in your faith. Let your children see the joy and fulfillment that comes from having friends who share your values and beliefs.

Ultimately, as we guide and nurture our children in a world filled with temptation, we must constantly point them back to God and His Word. Remind them that their worth and identity come from Him alone, and that true fulfillment can only be found in a relationship with Jesus Christ. Encourage your children to seek out friendships that will strengthen their faith and help them grow closer to God. By instilling these values in our children, we can help them navigate the challenges of peer pressure and stay true to their beliefs in a world that often seeks to lead them astray.

Cultural Shifts and Moral Relativism

In today's ever-changing world, cultural shifts can have a profound impact on our children's moral compass. As Christian parents, it is essential to address these shifts head on and instill in our children a strong foundation of faith and values. One of the most challenging aspects of navigating these cultural shifts is the rise of moral relativism, the belief that there are no absolute moral truths. This can lead to confusion and moral ambiguity for our children, making it more important than ever to provide them with a solid grounding in God's truth.

It is crucial for us as parents to teach our children the importance of standing firm in their beliefs, even when the world around them may be telling them otherwise. By nurturing their faith and guiding them with love and understanding, we can help them navigate the challenges of moral relativism and stay true to their Christian values. This means having open and honest conversations with our children about the cultural shifts they may encounter and equipping them with the tools they need to make wise and godly decisions.

As we raise our children in a world that often seems to be moving further away from God, it can be easy to feel discouraged. However, we must remember that God is always with us, guiding and strengthening us as we navigate these challenges. By focusing on the positive aspects of our faith and the power of prayer, we can find comfort and hope in knowing that God is in control. Our children look to us as role models, and by demonstrating a strong faith and unwavering commitment to God's truth, we can inspire them to do the same.

In a society that promotes moral relativism and shifting values, it can be easy for our children to feel lost and uncertain about what is right and wrong. As Christian parents, it is our duty to provide them with a solid foundation of faith and values that will guide them through life's challenges. By modeling godly behavior, fostering open communication, and nurturing a strong relationship with God, we can help our children navigate the cultural shifts of our time with confidence and grace.

In conclusion, cultural shifts and moral relativism may present challenges for our children, but with God's guidance and our unwavering support, they can navigate these challenges with strength and integrity. By nurturing their faith, teaching them to stand firm in their beliefs, and providing them with a strong foundation of values, we can raise godly children who will shine brightly in a world filled with temptation. Let us continue to trust in God's plan for our families and lean on Him for wisdom and guidance as we navigate the ever changing landscape of our culture.

The world is changing, and more people claim that right and wrong depend on the situation. But the Bible teaches absolute truths that do not change.

Self-Centered Thinking: Modern culture often prioritizes personal happiness and desires, whereas the Bible teaches us to think of others.

Self-centered thinking is a prevalent mindset in today's modern culture. It is easy to get caught up in prioritizing our personal happiness and desires above all else. However, as Christian parents and adults, we are called to a higher standard. The Bible teaches us to think of others and to consider their needs above our own. This is a fundamental principle that we must instill in our children from a young age.

In a world that constantly bombards us with messages of self-gratification and instant gratification, it can be challenging to resist the temptation to focus solely on ourselves. But as parents, we have the opportunity to model selfless behavior for our children. By demonstrating acts of kindness, generosity, and compassion towards others, we can show our children the importance of putting others first.

Teaching our children to think of others not only aligns with biblical teachings but also helps them develop empathy and compassion for those around them. When we encourage our children to consider the feelings and needs of others, we are helping them cultivate a heart of service and love. This mindset sets them apart from the self-centered attitudes that prevail in society and equips them to be a light in a world that desperately needs it.

As Christian parents and adults, we have a responsibility to nurture and guide our children in the ways of the Lord. This includes teaching them to resist the temptation of self- centered thinking and to prioritize the well-being of others. By instilling these values in our children, we are equipping them to live out their faith in a tangible way and to make a positive impact on the world around them.

So let us strive to cultivate a culture of selflessness and love in our homes and communities. Let us teach our children the importance of thinking of others and modeling this behavior in our own lives. Together, we can raise a generation of godly children who shine brightly in a world that desperately needs the light of Christ.

Materialism: Media and advertisements promote the idea that happiness comes from possessions, but true contentment comes from God.

In today's society, materialism is a prevalent mindset that is constantly reinforced by the media and advertisements. We are bombarded with messages telling us that happiness comes from possessions, and that we must have the latest gadgets, fashion trends, and luxury items in order to feel truly content. However, as Christian parents and adults, we must remember that true contentment comes from God, not from material possessions.

It is important to teach our children the difference between temporary happiness derived from material possessions and lasting contentment found in our relationship with God. By instilling in them the values of gratitude, humility, and faith, we can help them resist the pressures of consumerism and materialism that surround them. Encourage them to find joy in the simple things in life, such as spending time with loved ones, enjoying nature, and serving others in need.

As parents, we must lead by example and show our children that true happiness does not come from accumulating wealth or possessions, but from cultivating a strong faith and relationship with God. By prioritizing our spiritual growth and nurturing our connection with God, we can demonstrate to our children where true contentment lies. Encourage them to seek fulfillment in their faith, rather than in material possessions that will ultimately leave them feeling empty and unsatisfied.

In a world that constantly bombards us with messages of consumerism and materialism; it can be challenging to raise children who prioritize their spiritual well-being over material possessions. However, by creating a loving and supportive environment rooted in faith, we can help our children develop a strong sense of self-worth and contentment that does not rely on external factors. Encourage them to find joy in their relationship with God, and to trust in His provision and guidance as they navigate the temptations of the world.

As Christian parents and adults, let us remember that our ultimate goal is to nurture godly children who find true contentment in their faith and relationship with God. By teaching them to resist the allure of material possessions and to prioritize their spiritual growth, we can help them navigate the challenges of a materialistic world with grace and wisdom.

Encourage them to seek fulfillment in their faith, and to trust that true happiness comes from knowing and serving a loving God who provides for all our needs.

Tips for Parents

As Christian parents, we are called to raise our children in a world that often goes against the values and teachings of our faith. It can be challenging to navigate the temptations and influences that surround our children, but with God's guidance and our steadfast commitment, we can nurture godly children even in an ungodly world. Here are some tips to help you on this journey:

First and foremost, lead by example. Your children are always watching and learning from you, so it's important to model the behavior and values that you want them to emulate.

Show them what it means to live a life of faith, integrity, and compassion. Let your actions speak louder than your words and demonstrate the love of Christ in all that you do.

Secondly, create a strong foundation of prayer in your home. Teach your children the importance of talking to God, seeking His guidance, and relying on His strength. Encourage them to develop their own relationship with God through prayer, Bible study, and worship.

Pray together as a family and lift each other up in times of joy and struggle.

Thirdly, prioritize open communication with your children. Create a safe and welcoming environment where they feel comfortable sharing their thoughts, feelings, and questions. Listen attentively, validate their emotions, and offer guidance and support without judgment. Help them navigate the challenges they face in the world with wisdom and grace.

Additionally, set clear boundaries and expectations for your children. Establish rules and consequences that are rooted in love and discipline. Consistency is key in enforcing these boundaries, but also allow room for grace and forgiveness. Help your children understand the reasons behind the rules and empower them to make wise choices on their own.

Lastly, surround your family with a community of faith. Connect with other Christian families, church members, and mentors who can provide support, encouragement, and accountability. Share your struggles and victories with one another, and pray for one another's children. Together, we can strengthen each other in our shared mission of raising godly children in an ungodly world.

Understanding these influences can help you protect your kids' faith. Here are some practical steps: Monitor Media Consumption: Pay attention to what your kids watch and play, ensuring it aligns with biblical values.

As Christian parents, it is essential to monitor the media consumption of our children and ensure that what they watch and play aligns with biblical values. In today's world, there is an abundance of media content that can easily lead our children astray from God's teachings. By paying attention to what our kids are exposed to, we can help guide them to- wards a path of righteousness and instill in them a strong foundation of faith.

One of the first steps in monitoring media consumption is to be aware of the content that is being presented to our children. This means taking the time to research and understand the messages and values that are being portrayed in movies, TV shows, video games, and other forms of media. By being proactive in our approach, we can better protect our children from being influenced by harmful or inappropriate content.

It is also important to engage in open and honest conversations with our children about the media they consume. By discussing the content they are watching or playing, we can help them develop a discerning eye and teach them to critically evaluate the messages they are being exposed to. Encourage your children to ask questions and express their thoughts and feelings about what they are consuming, so they can begin to understand the importance of aligning their media choices with biblical values.

Furthermore, setting boundaries and guidelines for media consumption is crucial in shaping our children's worldview. Establishing limits on screen time, restricting access to certain types of content, and encouraging wholesome alternatives can help create a safe and nurturing environment for our children to grow in their faith. By being intentional and consistent in enforcing these boundaries, we can help our children develop a discerning taste for media that upholds biblical values.

In conclusion, monitoring media consumption is a vital aspect of nurturing godly children in an ungodly world. By paying attention to what our kids watch and play, engaging in meaningful conversations, setting boundaries, and leading by example, we can guide our children towards a life that is rooted in faith and aligned with God's teachings. Let us commit to being vigilant in our efforts to protect and nurture the hearts and minds of our children, so they may grow up to be strong and steadfast followers of Christ.

Open Communication: Discuss what they learn and who their friends are, using these conversations to teach biblical truths.

In today's society, it is more important than ever for Christian parents to have open communication with their children. By discussing what they are learning and who their friends are, parents can use these conversations to teach biblical truths and instill godly values in their children. This subchapter focuses on the importance of open communication in Nurturing Godly Children in an Ungodly World.

When parents take the time to discuss what their children are learning, they can help them navigate the often confusing and conflicting messages they are exposed to in school, on the internet, and through social media. By engaging in conversations about their education, parents can provide a biblical perspective on the subjects their children are studying and help them see how God's word applies to every aspect of their lives.

Similarly, knowing who their children's friends are is crucial in guiding them towards godly relationships. By talking with their children about their friends, parents can help them discern which relationships are healthy and which ones may lead them astray. By sharing biblical principles about friendship, parents can equip their children to make wise choices when it comes to the company they keep.

These conversations provide valuable opportunities for parents to impart biblical truths to their children in a way that is relevant and meaningful to them. By discussing real-life situations and applying scripture to them, parents can help their children see how God's word is not just a set of rules to follow, but a guide for living a fulfilling and purposeful life. By using these conversations to teach biblical truths, parents can help their children develop a strong foundation of faith that will sustain them through the challenges of growing up in an ungodly world.

In conclusion, open communication is a powerful tool for Nurturing Godly Children in an Ungodly World. By discussing what they learn and who their friends are, parents can use these conversations to teach biblical truths and help their children develop a strong faith that will guide them through life's challenges. Let us encourage one another as Christian parents to engage in meaningful conversations with our children, so that they may grow in wisdom and in the knowledge of God's love and grace.

Lead by Example: Model what it means to follow Jesus every day.

As Christian parents and adults, one of the most important ways we can nurture godly children in a world of temptation is by leading by example. Children are always watching and learning from the adults in their lives, so it is crucial that we model what it means to follow Jesus every day. This means living out our faith in a way that is authentic and consistent, showing our children what it looks like to walk closely with God.

One of the best ways to lead by example is by prioritizing time with God each day. This could mean starting your day with prayer and Bible reading, or finding moments throughout the day to connect with God in prayer. By making your relationship with God a priority, you show your children the importance of seeking God's guidance and wisdom in all areas of life.

Another way to model following Jesus is by demonstrating love and forgiveness in your relationships. Children learn how to treat others by watching how we interact with those around us. When we extend grace and forgiveness to others, we show our children the transformative power of Christ's love in our lives. By modeling forgiveness and reconciliation, we teach our children the importance of living out the gospel in our relationships.

Additionally, leading by example means living a life of integrity and honesty. Our actions should align with our beliefs, and our words should reflect the truth of the gospel. When we are honest and trustworthy in all areas of our lives, we show our children the importance of living a life of integrity and righteousness. By modeling honesty and integrity, we help our children understand the value of living a life that is pleasing to God.

In conclusion, leading by example is one of the most powerful ways we can nurture godly children in a world of temptation. By prioritizing time with God, demonstrating love and forgiveness, and living a life of integrity and honesty, we show our children what it means to follow Jesus every day. Let us strive to be living examples of Christ's love and grace, so that our children may be inspired to walk closely with God in their own lives.

Teach Critical Thinking: Help your kids discern truth by comparing what they encounter with biblical teachings.

Teaching critical thinking skills to our children is one of the most important tasks we have as Christian parents in today's world. With so many conflicting messages bombarding them from all sides, it is crucial that our children learn to discern truth from deception. By comparing everything they encounter with biblical teachings, they will be better equipped to navigate the challenges of life with a foundation of faith and wisdom.

As parents, we must lead by example and demonstrate the importance of critical thinking in our own lives. We can encourage our children to ask questions, seek out different perspectives, and think critically about the information they are exposed to. By engaging in open and honest discussions with them, we can help them develop the skills they need to evaluate the world around them through a biblical lens.

One way to help our children discern truth is to encourage them to compare what they hear, see, and read with the teachings of the Bible. By instilling in them a love for God's Word and a desire to seek His truth in all things, we can empower them to make wise decisions and resist the temptations of the world. When they encounter conflicting messages or questionable content, they can turn to the Bible for guidance and clarity.

In a world that is constantly changing and evolving, it is more important than ever to equip our children with the tools they need to navigate the complexities of life. By teaching them to think critically and compare everything they encounter with biblical teachings, we are preparing them to stand firm in their faith and resist the pressures of the world. As Christian parents, let us commit to nurturing our children in a way that honors God and equips them to live out their faith in a world of temptation.

In conclusion, teaching our children to think critically and compare everything they encounter with biblical teachings is a vital part of nurturing godly children in an ungodly world. By instilling in them a love for God's Word and a desire to seek His truth above all else, we are helping them develop the skills they need to discern truth from deception. Let us continue to lead by example, engage in open and honest discussions, and provide our children with a solid foundation of faith and wisdom. Together, we can raise up a generation of young people who are equipped to navigate the challenges of life with courage, integrity, and a steadfast commitment to following Christ.

Encourage Positive Friendships: Help them form friendships with peers who share their faith.

Encouraging positive friendships is crucial for nurturing godly children in an ungodly world. One way to do this is by helping your children form friendships with peers who share their faith. By surrounding them with like minded individuals, you are providing a strong support system that can help them stay grounded in their beliefs and values.

It is important for Christian parents to be intentional about the friendships their children form. Encouraging them to seek out friends who share their faith can help prevent them from being swayed by negative influences. By fostering relationships with peers who have similar beliefs, your children can grow in their faith and support each other in their spiritual journey.

One way to help your children form friendships with peers who share their faith is by getting involved in church activities and youth groups. By participating in these groups, your children can meet other young people who are also seeking to grow in their relationship with God. Encourage them to attend events and retreats where they can build lasting friendships with fellow believers.

Another way to encourage positive friendships is by modeling healthy relationships in your own life. Show your children the importance of surrounding themselves with people who uplift and encourage them in their faith. By demonstrating the value of strong friendships based on shared beliefs, you can help your children understand the significance of choosing friends who will support them in their spiritual journey.

In conclusion, helping your children form friendships with peers who share their faith is a powerful way to nurture them in a world filled with temptation. By encouraging positive relationships with like-minded individuals, you are providing

A strong foundation for your children to grow in their faith and resist negative influences. As Christian parents, it is our responsibility to guide our children in choosing friends who will uplift and encourage them in their walk with God.

By understanding the challenges your kids face, you can help them stay strong in their faith. This chapter is just the beginning of our journey in raising godly children.

In today's world, our children face countless challenges to their faith. From peer pressure to secular influences, the temptations are everywhere. As Christian parents, it is our responsibility to understand these challenges and help our children navigate them with strength and conviction. By being aware of the obstacles they may encounter, we can better equip them to stand firm in their beliefs.

One of the first steps in nurturing godly children is to have open and honest conversations with them about the struggles they may face. By creating a safe space for dialogue, we can help our children feel supported and understood. Encourage them to share their thoughts and feelings, and offer guidance and wisdom from a biblical perspective. By fostering a strong and trusting relationship with our children, we can help them develop a solid foundation in their faith.

Another important aspect of raising godly children is to model a strong faith ourselves. Our children look to us as role models, so it is crucial that we demonstrate our own commitment to God in our daily lives. By living out our faith authentically, we show our children the importance of put- ting God first in all things. Let your actions speak louder than your words, and let your children see the joy and peace that comes from a relationship with Christ.

As we embark on this journey of raising godly children, let us remember that it is a marathon, not a sprint. There will be ups and downs, victories and setbacks, but through it all, we must remain steadfast in our commitment to nurturing our children's faith. By leaning on God for strength and guidance, we can weather any storm that comes our way. Trust in His plan for your children, and have faith that He will equip you with everything you need to raise them in a way that honors Him.

This chapter is just the beginning of our journey in raising godly children. As we continue on this path, let us lean on one another for support and encouragement. Together, we can help our children stay strong in their faith and navigate the challenges of this world with grace and resilience. With God by our side, we can raise a generation of children who are firmly rooted in their beliefs and unshaken by the world's temptations.

CHAPTER TWO

BUILDING A STRONG SPIRITUAL FOUNDATION

*a*s Christian parents and adults, one of our greatest responsibilities is to build a strong spiritual foundation for the children in our care. In a world filled with temptation and distraction, it can be challenging to raise children who are grounded in their faith and equipped to navigate the complexities of life. However, with dedication and the guidance of the Holy Spirit, we can help our children grow into spiritually resilient individuals who are able to stand firm in their beliefs.

One of the key ways to build a strong spiritual foundation for our children is through consistent prayer and devotion. By setting aside time each day to pray with our children, we are modeling the importance of communication with God and inviting His presence into our homes. Encouraging our children to develop their own prayer life and seek God's guidance in all things will help them cultivate a deep and personal relationship with their Heavenly Father. Another essential aspect of building a strong spiritual foundation is teaching our children the Word of God. By regularly reading and studying the Bible together as a family, we are instilling in our children a love for God's Word and equipping them with the knowledge they need to navigate life's challenges. Encouraging our children to memorize key verses and apply biblical principles to their daily lives will help them develop a solid spiritual grounding that will sustain them in times of doubt and temptation.

In addition to prayer and Bible study, it is important to cultivate a spirit of worship and praise in our homes. By engaging in times of corporate worship as a family, we are creating an atmosphere where our children can experience the presence of God in a tangible way.

Encouraging our children to express their love and gratitude to God through music, song, and dance will help them develop a heart of worship that will sustain them through the trials and tribulations of life.

Ultimately, building a strong spiritual foundation for our children requires us to lead by example. By living out our faith authentically and demonstrating God's love and grace in our words and actions, we are showing our children what it means to be a follower of Christ. As we strive to be a positive influence in their lives and point them towards the truth of God's Word, we can trust that He will guide and protect them as they navigate the challenges of the world around them.

Creating a strong spiritual foundation for your children is essential for helping them grow in their faith. This foundation will guide them through life's challenges and help them stay rooted in their beliefs. In this chapter, we will explore practical ways to build this foundation, using simple steps and Bible references to guide you.

As Christian parents and adults, we understand the importance of nurturing our children in the ways of the Lord. It is our responsibility to provide them with a strong spiritual foundation that will help them navigate the challenges of life and stay rooted in their faith. In this chapter, we will explore practical ways to build this foundation, using simple steps and Bible references to guide you.

One of the first steps in creating a strong spiritual foundation for your children is to lead by example. Your children look to you as a role model, so it is essential that you demonstrate a strong faith and commitment to God in your own life. Show them through your actions and words what it means to live a life guided by faith and love.

Another important aspect of building a strong spiritual foundation for your children is to engage them in regular prayer and Bible study. Set aside time each day to pray together as a family and read from the Word of God. Encourage your children to ask questions and explore the teachings of the Bible with curiosity and an open heart.

In addition to prayer and Bible study, it is important to involve your children in the life of the church. Encourage them to participate in Sunday school, youth group activities, and community service projects. By actively engaging in the church community, your children will develop a sense of belonging and a deeper understanding of their faith.

Finally, teach your children the importance of living out their faith in their daily lives. Encourage them to show love and kindness to others, to stand up for what is right, and to trust in God's plan for their lives. By instilling these values in your children and modeling a strong faith yourself, you will help them build a solid spiritual foundation that will guide them through life's challenges and temptations.

The Importance of a Spiritual Foundation

In today's fast-paced and ever changing world, it can be challenging for Christian parents to raise godly children who stay true to their faith in the face of temptation. That's why it is crucial to establish a strong spiritual foundation for our children from a young age. This foundation serves as a solid anchor, guiding them through life's ups and downs and helping them navigate the many temptations that come their way.

One of the key reasons why a spiritual foundation is so important is that it provides children with a sense of purpose and direction. When they understand their identity as beloved children of God, they are less likely to be swayed by the pressures and influences of the world. Instead, they are able to make decisions based on their faith and values, leading them towards a life of fulfillment and meaning.

Furthermore, a strong spiritual foundation helps children develop a personal relationship with God. This relationship is the cornerstone of their faith and gives them the strength and courage to face whatever challenges come their way. By nurturing this connection through prayer, scripture reading, and regular church attendance, parents can help their children deepen their faith and trust in God's plan for their lives.

In addition, a spiritual foundation provides children with a moral compass that guides their behavior and decision-making. In a world where ethical standards seem to be constantly shifting, it is essential for children to have a firm foundation of right and wrong rooted in their faith. This foundation helps them make wise choices and resist the temptations that can lead them astray.

Ultimately, nurturing a strong spiritual foundation in our children is one of the greatest gifts we can give them. It equips them to navigate the complexities of life with grace and wisdom, and prepares them to be strong and steadfast followers of Christ. As Christian parents, let us commit to building this foundation in our children, knowing that it will sustain them through all the trials and temptations they may face in this ungodly world.

A strong spiritual foundation is like a solid rock that supports your children through all of life's ups and downs. Jesus talks about this in Matthew 7:24-25: "Therefore everyone who hears these words of mine and puts them into practice is like a wise man who built his house on the rock. The rain came down, the streams rose, and the winds blew and beat against that house; yet it did not fall, because it had its foundation on the rock."

In the journey of raising children in today's world, it is crucial to establish a strong spiritual foundation that will serve as a solid rock to support them through all of life's ups and downs. Just like the wise man who built his house on the rock in Matthew 7:24-25, we must ensure that our children are grounded in faith and equipped with the teachings of Jesus to withstand the storms of life.

As Christian parents and adults, we have the incredible responsibility of nurturing godly children in a world filled with temptation and distractions. It is our duty to instill in them the values and principles of our faith, so that they may navigate the challenges of the world with grace and strength. By building their foundation on the teachings of Jesus, we can provide them with a firm footing that will not crumble in the face of adversity.

The imagery of a house built on a rock is a powerful reminder of the importance of a strong spiritual foundation for our children. Just as a house with a solid rock foundation will not fall when the rain comes down and the winds blow, our children will be able to withstand the storms of life when their faith is deeply rooted in Christ. Through prayer, Bible study, and modeling a life of faith, we can help our children build a strong and unshakable foundation that will guide them throughout their lives.

It is easy to be discouraged by the challenges and temptations that our children face in today's world. However, we must remember that with a strong spiritual foundation, our children have the resilience and strength to overcome any obstacle that comes their way. As we guide and support them in their faith journey, we can take comfort in knowing that they are building their house on the rock of Christ's teachings, and that no storm can shake their foundation.

Let us continue to nurture our children in the ways of the Lord, knowing that a strong spiritual foundation is the key to helping them thrive in an ungodly world. With faith, love, and perseverance, we can equip our children to stand firm in their beliefs and walk boldly in the path that God has set before them. May we be encouraged by the promise that when our children's foundation is built on the rock of Christ, they will not fall, no matter what challenges they may face.

Teaching Your Children About God

As Christian parents, one of the most important responsibilities we have is to teach our children about God. In a world filled with temptation and worldly influences, it is crucial that we instill in our children a strong foundation of faith and values. By nurturing our children in the ways of the Lord, we are equipping them to navigate the challenges of life with wisdom and discernment.

One of the most effective ways to teach our children about God is through modeling a life of faith and devotion. Children learn by example, and when they see us living out our beliefs in our daily lives, they are more likely to embrace those beliefs themselves. This means making time for prayer, Bible study, and attending church as a family. By prioritizing our relationship with God, we are showing our children the importance of putting Him first in all things.

In addition to modeling a life of faith, it is important to engage our children in conversations about God and His Word. Take the time to read the Bible with your children, discuss its teachings, and answer any questions they may have. Encourage them to pray and seek God's guidance in all aspects of their lives. By fostering an open dialogue about faith, we are helping our children develop a personal relationship with God that will sustain them throughout their lives.

Another important aspect of teaching our children about God is helping them understand the concept of sin and forgiveness. It is crucial for children to recognize their need for a Savior and to understand the significance of Jesus' sacrifice on the cross. By teaching our children about God's grace and forgiveness, we are instilling in them a sense of humility and gratitude that will shape their character and relationships with others.

Above all, it is essential to pray for our children and entrust them to God's care. As we seek His guidance and wisdom in raising our children, we can trust that He will equip us with everything we need to nurture them in His ways. By teaching our children about God with love, patience, and consistency, we are laying a firm foundation for their spiritual growth and maturity.

Start by teaching your children about God and His love for them. Use simple language and share stories from the Bible. Bible Stories: Read stories from the Bible that show God's love and power, such as David and Goliath (1 Samuel 17) or Daniel in the lion's den (Daniel 6).

In the Bible, there are countless stories that showcase God's love and power, providing us with valuable lessons and inspiration. One such story is the classic tale of David and Goliath from 1 Samuel 17. This story teaches us that no matter how big our obstacles may seem, with God on our side, we can overcome anything. David, a young shepherd boy, faced the giant warrior Goliath with nothing but a slingshot and a stone. Through his unwavering faith in God, David defeated Goliath, showing us that faith and courage can lead to miraculous outcomes.

Another powerful story of God's love and protection is found in the account of Daniel in the lion's den from Daniel 6. Daniel, a faithful servant of God, was thrown into a den of hungry lions as punishment for his devotion to God. Despite the seemingly impossible circumstances, God protected Daniel from harm, shutting the mouths of the lions. This story reminds us that God is always with us, even in our darkest hours, and He is able to deliver us from any situation.

As Christian parents, it is important to share these Bible stories with our children to instill in them a strong faith and trust in God. By reading these stories together, we can teach our children about God's love, power, and faithfulness. We can show them that no matter what challenges they may face in life, God is always there to guide, protect, and strengthen them. By discussing these stories with our children, we can help them see that they are never alone and that God's love is always surrounding them. We can encourage them to have faith like David, facing their fears with courage and trust in God's provision. We can inspire them to be like Daniel, standing firm in their beliefs even when faced with opposition.

Through these stories, we can nurture our children's spiritual growth and equip them to navigate the temptations of an ungodly world with unwavering faith.

So let us take the time to read and reflect on these powerful Bible stories with our children, allowing God's love and power to transform their hearts and minds. Let us be intentional in teaching them about the incredible ways God works in the lives of His people, inspiring them to trust in Him whole- heartedly. Together, as Christian parents and adults, we can raise up a generation of children who are rooted in God's love, empowered by His strength, and equipped to shine brightly in a world filled with darkness.

Daily Devotions: Spend time each day reading a Bible verse and talking about what it means. Deuteronomy 6:6-7 says, "These commandments that I give you today are to be on your hearts. Impress them on your children. Talk about them when you sit at home and when you walk along the road, when you lie down and when you get up."

Daily devotions are a crucial aspect of raising children in a world filled with temptation. Taking the time each day to read a Bible verse and discuss its meaning with your children can help instill important values and beliefs in their hearts. Deuteronomy 6:6-7 reminds us of the importance of constantly impressing God's commandments on our children, whether we are at home, walking along the road, lying down, or getting up. By incorporating daily devotions into your family routine, you are actively nurturing your children's spiritual growth and helping them navigate the challenges of the world around them.

Setting aside time each day for devotions not only allows your children to develop a deeper understanding of God's word, but it also provides an opportunity for meaningful conversations about faith and values. By discussing the Bible verses you read together, you can help your children apply these teachings to their daily lives and make connections between scripture and real-world situations. This practice can strengthen their relationship with God and equip them with the tools they need to make wise choices in the face of temptation.

As Christian parents, it is our responsibility to guide our children in their faith journey and help them build a strong foundation in God's word. Daily devotions offer a structured and intentional way to nurture their spiritual development and reinforce the values and beliefs that are important to our family. By consistently engaging in these devotional times, we are demonstrating the importance of prioritizing our relationship with God and encouraging our children to do the same.

In a world that is constantly bombarding our children with messages that contradict our Christian beliefs, daily devotions serve as a powerful tool to counteract these negative influences. By immersing our children in God's word on a regular basis, we are equipping them with the knowledge and understanding they need to resist temptation and stand firm in their faith. These daily devotions can serve as a source of strength and guidance for our children as they navigate the challenges and pressures of the world around them.

In conclusion, daily devotions are an essential practice for nurturing godly children in an ungodly world. By spending time each day reading a Bible verse and discussing its meaning with our children, we are helping them grow in their faith and develop a strong foundation in God's word. Let us heed the words of Deuteronomy 6:6-7 and make daily devotions a priority in our families, so that we may raise children who are grounded in their faith and equipped to navigate the temptations of the world with wisdom and discernment.

Prayer

Prayer is a powerful tool that we, as Christian parents, can use to guide and protect our children in a world filled with temptation. It is through prayer that we can connect with God and seek His guidance in raising our children to be godly and righteous individuals. As we navigate the challenges of parenting in an ungodly world, prayer becomes our lifeline, providing us with strength, wisdom, and peace in the midst of chaos.

When we pray for our children, we are not only asking for God's protection and guidance, but we are also surrendering our fears and worries to Him. We are acknowledging that we cannot do this parenting journey alone, and that we need His help every step of the way.

Through prayer, we are inviting God into our homes and our hearts, allowing Him to work in and through us as we nurture our children in the ways of the Lord.

As Christian parents, it is important for us to model a life of prayer for our children. By incorporating prayer into our daily routines, we are showing our children the importance of seeking God's guidance and wisdom in all aspects of life. Whether it is praying together as a family before meals or bedtime, or setting aside time for personal prayer and reflection, we are teaching our children that prayer is a vital part of our relationship with God. In a world that is constantly bombarding our children with messages of materialism, selfishness, and immorality, prayer serves as a shield of protection around them. When we pray for our children's hearts and minds to be guarded against the influences of the world, we are asking God to fill them with His truth, love, and righteousness. Through prayer, we can instill in our children a deep sense of faith and resilience that will help them withstand the temptations and pressures they may face.

So let us not underestimate the power of prayer in nurturing our children in a world of temptation. Let us commit to lifting up our children in prayer daily, seeking God's guidance and protection over their lives. As we trust in God's faithfulness and love, we can rest assured that He is always with us, guiding us as we raise our children to be godly individuals in an ungodly world.

Teach your children to pray and make prayer a regular part of your family's life. Prayer is a way to communicate with God and grow closer to Him. Modeling Prayer: Pray with your children and let them see you pray. Jesus often prayed, showing us how important it is (Luke 5:16).

Modeling prayer is an essential aspect of nurturing godly children in today's ungodly world. As Christian parents and adults, it is crucial that we lead by example and show our children the importance of prayer in our daily lives. Jesus himself prayed regularly, setting an example for us to follow. In Luke 5:16, we are reminded of the significance of prayer in maintaining a close relationship with God. By praying with our children and letting them see us pray, we are teaching them how to communicate with God and seek His guidance in all aspects of their lives.

Praying with our children not only strengthens our own faith but also helps them develop a deeper understanding of the power of prayer. When they see us turning to God in times of need, they learn to do the same. By involving them in our prayers, we are instilling in them a sense of trust in God and a reliance on His wisdom and strength. Our children will learn to lean on God for guidance and support, knowing that He is always there to listen and respond to their prayers.

As parents, it is important to create a habit of prayer within our families. By setting aside time each day to pray together, we are demonstrating the value we place on seeking God's presence and guidance. This practice not only strengthens our bond with our children but also reinforces the importance of prayer in their lives. When they see us making prayer a priority, they are more likely to develop a habit of prayer themselves, turning to God in times of joy, sorrow, and uncertainty.

Prayer is a powerful tool that can help us navigate the challenges of raising godly children in a world filled with temptation. By modeling prayer for our children, we are equipping them with a spiritual foundation that will guide them through life's trials and tribulations.

Let us continue to pray with our children and show them the way to a deeper relationship with God. As we follow in the footsteps of Jesus, may our prayers be a source of strength and comfort for our families, grounding them in faith and love.

Simple Prayers: Teach your children simple prayers they can say, such as thanking God for their day or asking for help with a problem. Philippians 4:6 says, "Do not be anxious about anything, but in every situation, by prayer and petition, with thanksgiving, present your requests to God."

In the fast-paced and often chaotic world we live in, it can be easy for our children to feel overwhelmed or anxious. As Christian parents, it is our responsibility to teach our children the power of prayer and how it can bring them peace and comfort in times of trouble. One way to do this is by teaching them simple prayers that they can say throughout the day.

These prayers can be as short and sweet as, "Thank you God for this day," or "God, please help me with this problem I'm facing."

Philippians 4:6 reminds us not to be anxious about anything, but to present our requests to God with prayer and thanks- giving. This verse is a powerful reminder of the importance of turning to God in times of need and seeking His guidance and support. By instilling this practice in our children from a young age, we are helping them build a strong foundation of faith that will carry them through life's challenges.

Simple prayers may seem insignificant, but they can have a profound impact on our children's spiritual development. By teaching our children to pray regularly, we are helping them cultivate a personal relationship with

God and inviting Him into their daily lives. This practice can also serve as a reminder that they are never alone and that God is always there to listen and provide comfort.

As parents, it is important to model the act of prayer for our children. By praying with them and showing them the importance of seeking God's guidance in all things, we are demonstrating the power of faith and trust in God's plan. Encouraging our children to pray not only strengthens their own relationship with God but also reinforces the importance of faith in our family life.

So let us take the time to teach our children simple prayers that they can use to talk to God throughout the day. Let us show them the beauty and power of prayer and remind them that God is always listening and ready to help. As we nurture our children in the ways of the Lord, may we also be reminded of the truth in Philippians 4:6 that through prayer and thanksgiving, we can find peace and strength in any situation.

Worship

In the journey of nurturing godly children in a world filled with temptation, one of the most important aspects to focus on is the practice of worship. As Christian parents and adults, it is our responsibility to instill in our children a deep reverence and love for God through regular worship. Worship is not just about attending church on

Sundays, but it is a lifestyle of honoring and glorifying God in everything we do.

When we teach our children the importance of worship, we are helping them to develop a strong and lasting relationship with God. Through worship, we acknowledge God's sovereignty, express our gratitude for His blessings, and seek His guidance and strength in our daily lives. It is a time to come before the Lord with open hearts and minds, ready to receive His love and grace.

As parents, we can model a life of worship for our children by setting aside time each day for personal devotions and prayer. We can also involve them in family worship times, where we gather together to sing praises to God, read His word, and pray as a family. These moments of worship not only strengthen our own faith but also plant seeds of faith in the hearts of our children.

In a world that often prioritizes material wealth, success, and pleasure, teaching our children the value of worship helps them to keep their focus on what truly matters their relationship with God. By nurturing a heart of worship in our children, we are equipping them to resist the temptations of the world and to live a life that is pleasing to God. Let us encourage our children to worship God in spirit and in truth, knowing that He is worthy of all our praise and adoration.

May we, as Christian parents and adults, continue to guide and support our children in their journey of faith, leading by example and nurturing a love for worship in their hearts. Let us remind them that true fulfillment and joy can only be found in a close and intimate relationship with God, and that worship is the key to experiencing His presence in our lives. As we cultivate a culture of worship in our families, we are sowing seeds of faith that will bear fruit for generations to come.

Worship is another key part of building a strong spiritual foundation. It helps children focus on God and remember His greatness. Attending Church: Take your children to church regularly so they can learn about God and worship Him with others. Hebrews 10:25 reminds us not to give up meeting together.

Attending church regularly with your children is essential in nurturing their faith and helping them grow closer to God. Hebrews 10:25 reminds us of the importance of not giving up meeting together, as it is through gathering with other believers that we can encourage one another in our faith journey. By taking your children to church, you are providing them with the opportunity to learn about God, worship Him with others, and be surrounded by a community of believers who will support and uplift them.

When you take your children to church, you are showing them the value of prioritizing their relationship with God. By making church attendance a regular part of their routine, you are instilling in them the importance of setting aside time to worship and learn about God. This foundation will help them navigate the challenges and temptations of the world, knowing that they can always turn to God for guidance and strength.

Attending church as a family also provides a unique opportunity for bonding and connection. Sharing in worship and learning together can strengthen the family unit and create lasting memories that your children will cherish. By attending church as a family, you are modeling the importance of faith and community, and showing your children that God is at the center of your family life.

As Christian parents, it is our responsibility to nurture our children's faith and provide them with the tools they need to navigate the challenges of an ungodly world. By taking your children to church regularly, you are equipping them with a strong foundation in their faith that will guide them throughout their lives. Encourage your children to actively participate in church activities, such as Sunday school and youth group, so they can deepen their understanding of God and form lasting relationships with other believers.

In conclusion, attending church with your children is a vital aspect of nurturing their faith in a world filled with temptation. By following the guidance of Hebrews 10:25 and not giving up meeting together, you are providing your children with a solid foundation in their relationship with God. Embrace the opportunity to worship and learn alongside your children, and watch as their faith grows and flourishes in the nurturing environment of the church community.

Singing Praises: Sing worship songs at home and teach your children to praise God through music. Psalm 100:1-2 says, "Shout for joy to the Lord, all the earth. Worship the Lord with gladness; come before him with joyful songs."

In a world filled with distractions and temptations, it can be challenging to raise children who are grounded in their faith. However, one powerful way to instill a love for God in your children is through music. The Bible tells us in Psalm 100:1-2 to "Shout for joy to the Lord, all the earth. Worship the Lord with gladness; come before him with joyful songs." What better way to teach your children to praise God than through singing worship songs at home?

Singing praises to God not only brings joy and peace to our hearts, but it also helps to create a sense of unity and connection within the family. By making music a regular part of your family routine, you are setting a beautiful example for your children to follow.

Encourage them to sing along with you, to clap their hands, and to dance with joy as they worship the Lord.

As Christian parents, it is our responsibility to nurture our children's spiritual growth and teach them the importance of praising God. By incorporating worship songs into your daily routine, you are helping to create a strong foundation of faith that will carry them through life's challenges. Take the time to explain the lyrics of the songs to your children, so they understand the meaning behind the words they are singing.

Music has a way of touching our souls in a unique and powerful manner. By teaching your children to praise God through music, you are giving them a gift that will stay with them for a lifetime. Encourage them to use their voices to glorify God and to share His love with others. As they grow in their faith, they will find comfort and strength in the songs they have learned to sing.

So, Christian parents, take the time to sing praises to God with your children. Create a space in your home where worship songs are a regular part of your family's routine. Teach your children to praise God through music and watch as their faith grows and blossoms in the presence of the Lord. Remember, Psalm 100:1-2 reminds us to "Shout for joy to the Lord, all the earth. Worship the Lord with gladness; come before him with joyful songs." Let your home be filled with the beautiful sound of worship as you nurture your children in a world of temptation.

Living Out Your Faith

Living out your faith is essential in Nurturing Godly Children in an Ungodly World. As Christian parents and adults, our actions and behaviors speak volumes to our children and those around us. It is important to not only talk the talk but walk the walk when it comes to living out our faith. Our children are watching and learning from us, so it is crucial that we set a positive example for them to follow.

One way to live out your faith is by being intentional about incorporating God into every aspect of your life. This means praying together as a family, reading the Bible regularly, and attending church services. By making God a priority in your daily routine, you are showing your children the importance of faith and how it can guide them through life's challenges.

Another way to live out your faith is by serving others and showing love and compassion to those in need. Jesus taught us to love our neighbors as ourselves, and by following this commandment, we are demonstrating the true essence of Christianity to our children.

Encourage your children to volunteer at local charities or participate in mission trips to help those less fortunate. By doing so, you are instilling in them a sense of empathy and kindness that will carry them throughout their lives.

Living out your faith also means being a light in a world filled with darkness. In a society that often promotes selfishness and materialism, it is important to show your children the joy and fulfillment that comes from living a life of faith. By choosing to prioritize God over worldly desires, you are demonstrating to your children the true source of happiness and contentment.

In conclusion, living out your faith is not always easy, but it is necessary in order to raise godly children in a world of temptation. By being intentional about incorporating God into every aspect of your life, serving others, and being a light in a dark world, you are setting a positive example for your children to follow. Remember, your actions speak louder than words, so let your faith shine brightly for all to see.

Show your children what it means to live out their faith in everyday life. Be an example they can follow. Kindness and Love: Show kindness and love to others, just as Jesus did. John 13:34 says, "A new command I give you:

Love one another. As I have loved you, so you must love one another."

Kindness and love are two powerful virtues that can have a profound impact on the world around us. As Christian parents and adults, it is our responsibility to teach our children the importance of showing kindness and love to others, just as Jesus did. In John 13:34, Jesus gives us a new commandment to love one another as He has loved us. This commandment serves as a reminder of the incredible love that Jesus has for each and every one of us, and it challenges us to extend that same love to those around us.

When we show kindness and love to others, we are reflecting the love of Christ in our lives. Our actions speak louder than words, and when we demonstrate love and kindness in our interactions with others, we are setting a powerful example for our children to follow. By showing compassion, forgiveness, and understanding to those around us, we are spreading the message of God's love and grace to a world that is in desperate need of it.

As we navigate the challenges of raising godly children in an ungodly world, it is important to remember the impact that our actions and words can have on those around us. By choosing to show kindness and love in all situations, we are not only honoring God's commandment to love one another, but we are also creating a positive and nurturing environment for our children to grow and thrive in. Our children are watching and learning from us, and by modeling Christ like behavior, we are equipping them with the tools they need to navigate the complexities of the world around them.

In a world filled with temptation and negativity, it can be easy to become discouraged and lose sight of the importance of showing kindness and love to others. However, as followers of Christ, we are called to be a light in the darkness and to demonstrate the transformative power of God's love through our actions and words. By making a conscious effort to show kindness and love to those around us, we are not only fulfilling God's commandment to love one another, but we are also making a positive impact on the lives of those we encounter.

Let us embrace the challenge of showing kindness and love to others, just as Jesus did. Let us be intentional in our interactions with those around us, and let us strive to reflect the love of Christ in all that we do. By nurturing a spirit of kindness and love in our own lives, we are not only shaping the hearts and minds of our children, but we are also spreading God's love to a world that is in desperate need of it.

Helping Others: Involve your children in acts of service, like helping a neighbor or volunteering. Galatians 5:13 says, "Serve one another humbly in love."

In this subchapter, we will explore the importance of involving our children in acts of service. As Christian parents, it is our responsibility to teach our children the value of helping others and serving one another. Galatians 5:13 reminds us to serve one another humbly in love, and what better way to demonstrate this to our children than by involving them in acts of service.

By involving our children in acts of service, we not only instill in them the importance of helping others, but we also teach them valuable life skills and lessons. Volunteering and helping a neighbor can help our children develop empathy, compassion, and a sense of responsibility towards others. These are qualities that are essential for nurturing godly children in an ungodly world.

When we involve our children in acts of service, we are also setting a positive example for them to follow. Children learn by watching and imitating their parents, so when they see us serving others with humility and love, they are more likely to do the same. By involving our children in acts of service, we are not only teaching them to be kind and compassionate individuals, but we are also helping them grow in their faith and understanding of what it means to follow Christ.

There are many ways in which we can involve our children in acts of service. Whether it is volunteering at a local soup kitchen, helping a neighbor with yard work, or participating in a mission trip, there are countless opportunities for our children to serve others and make a positive impact in their community. By involving our children in acts of service, we are not only helping them grow spiritually, but we are also helping them develop a heart for others and a desire to make a difference in the world.

So let us take to heart the words of Galatians 5:13 and serve one another humbly in love. Let us involve our children in acts of service and teach them the joy that comes from helping others. Together, as Christian parents and adults, we can nurture godly children in an ungodly world and raise up a generation of compassionate, kind-hearted individuals who shine the light of Christ wherever they go.

Creating a God-Centered Home

Creating a God-centered home is essential in nurturing godly children in a world filled with temptation. As Christian parents, it is our responsibility to cultivate an environment that reflects our faith and values. By centering our home around God, we can instill in our children a strong foundation of faith that will guide them through the challenges they may face in an ungodly world.

One way to create a God-centered home is to prioritize prayer and scripture study as a family. Make time each day to gather together for prayer and to read and discuss passages from the Bible. This practice not only strengthens your own faith but also sets an example for your children to follow. Encourage them to ask questions and engage in meaningful conversations about their beliefs and how they can apply them in their daily lives.

Another important aspect of creating a God-centered home is to model Christ like behavior in all that you do. Show love, kindness, and forgiveness to others, and teach your children to do the same. By demonstrating these virtues, you are teaching your children how to live out their faith in a practical way. Remember that your actions speak louder than words, so strive to be a positive role model for your children in all aspects of your life.

In addition to prayer, scripture study, and modeling Christ like behavior, it is important to surround your family with a community of like-minded believers. Regularly attending church services, participating in Bible studies, and engaging in fellowship with other Christian families can help reinforce the values you are teaching at home. Encourage your children to build relationships with other children who share their faith, as this can provide them with a strong support system as they navigate the challenges of an ungodly world.

Ultimately, creating a God-centered home is a lifelong journey that requires dedication, perseverance, and faith. Trust in God's guidance as you strive to raise your children in a way that honors Him. Remember that you are not alone in this endeavor, and that God is always with you, providing you with the strength and wisdom you need to nurture godly children in a world of temptation. Stay encouraged, stay faithful, and trust in God's plan for your family.

Make your home a place where faith is a natural part of daily life. Surround your children with reminders of God's love and teachings. Family Bible Time: Set aside time each week for a family Bible study. Talk about what you read and how you can apply it to your lives.

Welcome to the subchapter on Family Bible Time! In today's fast paced world, it can be challenging to find time to sit down and connect as a family. However, setting aside a specific time each week for a family Bible study can be incredibly beneficial for nurturing godly children. By reading and discussing scripture together, you are not only strengthening your family bond but also instilling important values and teachings in your children.

When planning your family Bible time, choose a time that works best for your family schedule. Whether it's after dinner on a weeknight or Sunday mornings before church, find a time that allows everyone to be present and engaged. Make it a priority and treat it as a special time for your family to come together and grow in faith.

During your family Bible time, encourage open discussions about what you read. Ask your children how they interpret the scripture and how they think it can be applied to their lives. Share your own insights and experiences to help guide the conversation. By actively engaging in these discussions, you are not only teaching your children about the Bible but also showing them how to apply its teachings in their daily lives.

As you continue to have regular family Bible time, consider incorporating activities or lessons that align with the scripture you are studying. This could include journaling, creating art, or even acting out a parable. By making the Bible study interactive and engaging, you are helping your children better understand and remember the lessons learned from scripture.

In conclusion, family Bible time is a wonderful way to nurture godly children in an ungodly world. By setting aside dedicated time each week to study scripture together, you are creating a foundation of faith and values that will guide your children throughout their lives. Remember, the family that prays and studies together, stays together. So, make it a priority to have regular family Bible time and watch as your children grow in their faith and understanding of God's word.

Faith Symbols: Decorate your home with Bible verses and faith based artwork to remind your family of God's presence.

In a world filled with distractions and temptations, it can be easy for our children to lose sight of their faith. As Christian parents and adults, it is our responsibility to create a home environment that nurtures and strengthens our children's relationship with God. One way to do this is by incorporating faith symbols into our decor. By surrounding our families with Bible verses and faith-based artwork, we can create a constant reminder of God's presence in our lives.

Decorating your home with Bible verses is a simple yet powerful way to infuse your space with the word of God. Choose verses that are meaningful to your family and display them prominently in common areas such as the living room, kitchen, or bedrooms. These verses can serve as daily reminders of God's love, wisdom, and promises, helping to reinforce your family's faith and values.

In addition to Bible verses, consider incorporating faith- based artwork into your home decor. Whether it's a beautiful painting of Jesus, a cross, or a scene from the Bible, these pieces can serve as visual reminders of your family's beliefs and values. Displaying faith based artwork in your home can create a peaceful and uplifting atmosphere, helping to inspire and encourage your children in their faith journey.

As you decorate your home with faith symbols, take the time to explain the significance of each piece to your children. Share the stories behind the Bible verses and artwork, and discuss how they relate to your family's beliefs and values. Encourage your children to ask questions and engage in discussions about their faith, helping them to deepen their understanding and connection to God.

By surrounding your family with faith symbols, you are creating a nurturing and supportive environment that will help your children grow in their faith and relationship with God. Let your home be a sanctuary of faith, filled with reminders of God's presence and love.

Together, we can raise godly children in an ungodly world, guiding them on a path of faith, hope, and love.

By taking these steps, you can help your children build a strong spiritual foundation that will support them throughout their lives. Remember, it's not about being perfect but about consistently pointing your children to God and His love for them.

As Christian parents and adults, we have a responsibility to nurture our children in their faith and help them build a strong spiritual foundation that will guide them throughout their lives. By taking intentional steps, we can instill in them a deep connection to God and His love. It's important to remember that we don't have to be perfect in our efforts, but rather consistent in pointing our children towards God and His teachings.

One of the first steps in helping our children build a strong spiritual foundation is to model a genuine relationship with God ourselves. Children learn by example, so it's crucial that we show them what it looks like to prioritize prayer, Bible study, and fellowship with other believers. By demonstrating our own faith in action, we can inspire our children to develop their own personal relationship with God.

Another key step in nurturing our children's spiritual growth is to create a home environment that is centered around faith. This can include incorporating regular family devotions, attending church together, and engaging in conversations about God and His teachings. By making faith a central part of our family life, we can help our children see the importance of prioritizing their relationship with God.

In addition to modeling a strong faith and creating a faith-centered home environment, we can also provide our children with opportunities to grow in their own spiritual journey. This can involve enrolling them in Sunday school or youth group, encouraging them to participate in church activities, and supporting them as they explore their own beliefs and questions about God. By giving our children the tools and resources they need to deepen their faith, we can empower them to build a strong spiritual foundation that will sustain them in the face of life's challenges.

By taking these steps to nurture our children's faith, we can help them build a strong spiritual foundation that will sup- port them throughout their lives. Remember, it's not about being perfect, but about consistently pointing our children to God and His love for them. As Christian parents and adults, let's commit to guiding our children in their faith journey and equipping them with the tools they need to navigate the temptations of this world with grace and strength.

CHAPTER THREE

BE THEIR PARENT, NOT THEIR FRIEND

*a*s Christian parents, it is crucial to remember that our primary role is to be a parent to our children, not just their friend. While it may be tempting to want to be their buddy and avoid conflict, our children need us to be their guide, their protector, and their disciplinarian.

Being their parent means setting boundaries, enforcing rules, and teaching them right from wrong in a loving and consistent manner.

One of the most important aspects of being a parent, rather than just a friend, is instilling in our children a strong moral compass rooted in our faith. We must teach them the values and principles of Christianity, and model those values in our own lives. By being a parent who leads by example, we can help our children navigate the challenges and temptations of an ungodly world with confidence and grace.

Being a parent also means being willing to have difficult conversations with our children about tough topics such as sex, drugs, and peer pressure. While these conversations may be uncomfortable, they are necessary for equipping our children to make wise choices and resist the pressures of the world around them. By being open and honest with our children, we can build trust and strengthen our relationship with them.

It is important to remember that being a parent, not a friend, does not mean being harsh or authoritarian. We can still show love, compassion, and understanding to our children while also holding them accountable for their actions. By setting clear expectations and consequences, we can help our children learn responsibility and develop self-discipline.

In conclusion, as Christian parents, we have been entrusted with the precious task of raising our children in a world that often goes against our beliefs. By being their parent, not just their friend, we can guide them with wisdom and love, helping them grow into godly individuals who will shine brightly in a dark and tempting world. Let us embrace this role whole- heartedly, knowing that we are not alone in this journey but have God's guidance and strength every step of the way.

One of the most important lessons I have learned as a parent is the need to be a parent first, and not a friend, until the right time comes to transition into that role. Our children naturally desire our friendship. They want our approval and companionship. However, there are times when our role as a parent requires us to make decisions that might not align with their immediate desires. This can lead to moments when our children express their frustration by saying, "You are no longer my friend."

It is essential to remember that our primary responsibility as parents is to guide and protect our children, even if it means making tough decisions that they may not understand or appreciate in the moment. We must remember that our ultimate goal is to raise children who are grounded in their faith and equipped to navigate the challenges of an ungodly world. This often requires us to set boundaries and make decisions that may not always be popular with our children.

As Christian parents, we are called to lead by example and instill in our children the values and principles of our faith. This means that sometimes we have to make decisions that go against the grain of what society may deem acceptable or popular. It is important to remember that our children may not always understand the reasons behind our decisions, but it is our duty to stand firm in our convictions and trust that God will guide us in raising our children with wisdom and discernment.

While it may be difficult to hear our children say, "You are no longer my friend," it is important to remember that our role as a parent is not to be their friend, but their guide and protector. We must trust that our children will come to appreciate the boundaries we have set and the decisions we have made in their best interest. It is through our unwavering commitment to nurturing godly children that we can help them navigate the challenges of an ungodly world with courage, faith, and grace.

In the end, being a parent first and a friend second is a challenging but necessary aspect of raising children in a world filled with temptation. By setting boundaries, making tough decisions, and standing firm in our faith, we can raise children who are grounded in their beliefs and equipped to navigate the trials and tribulations of life. Let us embrace our role as parents with love, patience, and trust in God's guidance as we nurture godly children in an ungodly world.

This sentiment is not unusual. Children often test boundaries and seek autonomy as they grow. They might react negatively when we set limits or enforce rules. But it is precisely in these moments that our role as a parent becomes crucial. Our children need guidance, discipline, and structure to navigate life's challenges and develop into responsible, well-rounded adults.

This sentiment is not unusual. Children often test boundaries and seek autonomy as they grow. It is a natural part of their development to push against limits and rules set by their parents. While it may be challenging to deal with their negative reactions, it is important to remember that as parents, our role is crucial in guiding them through these moments. By providing guidance, discipline, and structure, we are helping our children navigate life's challenges and grow into responsible, well-rounded adults.

As Christian parents, we have a unique opportunity to instill godly values and principles in our children. By setting boundaries and enforcing rules, we are teaching them the importance of obedience and respect. It is through these lessons that they learn to trust in God's plan for their lives and develop a strong moral compass to guide them through the temptations of the world.

When our children react negatively to the limits we set, it can be tempting to give in or avoid confrontation. However, it is in these moments that our consistency and firmness are most important. By standing firm in our decisions and enforcing consequences for their actions, we are teaching our children the importance of accountability and self-control.

It is not easy to be the disciplinarian, but it is a necessary part of parenting. Our children need structure and boundaries to feel secure and develop a sense of responsibility. By providing them with a safe and consistent environment, we are helping them grow into confident individuals who can navigate the challenges of life with grace and integrity.

In the end, our goal as Christian parents is to raise children who are grounded in their faith and equipped to face the temptations of the world with courage and conviction. By providing them with guidance, discipline, and structure, we are preparing them to live out their faith in a world that often seeks to lead them astray. Let us embrace our role as parents with love, patience, and a steadfast commitment to nurturing our children into godly individuals.

The Bible offers wisdom on the importance of discipline and guidance. In Proverbs 22:6, it says, "Train ups a child in the way he should go; even when he is old he will not depart from it." This verse highlights the long-term impact of the lessons and values we impart during our children's formative years. Our role is to provide a foundation that will support them throughout their lives.

In the book "Nurturing Godly Children in an Ungodly World," we are reminded of the wisdom found in the Bible regarding the importance of discipline and guidance in raising children. Proverbs 22:6 teaches us to train up our children in the way they should go, knowing that the lessons we instill in them during their formative years will stay with them for a lifetime. As Christian parents and adults, it is our responsibility to lay a strong foundation of values and principles that will support our children as they navigate through the challenges of an ungodly world.

We live in a society where temptations and distractions are constantly bombarding our children, pulling them away from the path of righteousness. However, as believers, we can find comfort in knowing that God's Word provides us with the tools and guidance we need to help our children stay on the right track. By instilling biblical principles and values in our children, we equip them with the necessary armor to resist the temptations that surround them.

It is important for us, as Christian parents and adults, to lead by example and demonstrate the importance of discipline and guidance in our own lives. Our children learn best through observation and imitation, so it is crucial that we model the values and behaviors we wish to instill in them. By living out our faith authentically and intentionally, we show our children the importance of walking in obedience to God's Word.

As we navigate the challenges of nurturing godly children in an ungodly world, we must remember that we are not alone in this journey. God is with us every step of the way, providing us with the strength, wisdom, and guidance we need to raise our children according to His will. Let us lean on Him for support and trust in His promises as we strive to train up our children in the way they should go.

In conclusion, let us embrace the wisdom found in Proverbs 22:6 and take to heart the importance of discipline and guidance in raising our children. By investing in their spiritual growth and equipping them with the tools they need to navigate through a world filled with temptation, we are laying a strong foundation that will support them throughout their lives. May we continue to seek God's wisdom and guidance as we nurture our children to become godly individuals in an ungodly world.

Furthermore, Hebrews 12:11 states, "No discipline seems pleasant at the time, but painful. Later on, however, it produces a harvest of righteousness and peace for those who have been trained by it." This passage acknowledges the temporary discomfort that discipline might cause but underscores the positive outcomes that result from it. As parents, it is our duty to endure these moments of discomfort for the greater good of our children's development.

Furthermore, Hebrews 12:11 reminds us that discipline is not always easy, but it is necessary for the growth and development of our children. As parents, we must be willing to endure the temporary discomfort that discipline may bring in order to see the long-term benefits it can provide. Just as a farmer must endure the hard work of tending to his crops in order to reap a bountiful harvest, so too must we be willing to put in the effort to nurture our children in the ways of righteousness.

This passage also serves as a reminder that discipline is an essential part of our children's training. Just as a coach pushes their athletes to their limits in order to help them reach their full potential, so too must we push our children to grow and develop in their faith. It may not always be pleasant in the moment, but the rewards of a disciplined and well- trained child are immeasurable.

As Christian parents, we have been entrusted with the responsibility of raising our children in the ways of the Lord. This means that we must be willing to discipline them when necessary, even if it means facing their displeasure in the short term. By doing so, we are helping to shape them into the righteous and peaceful individuals that God has called them to be.

In a world filled with temptation and sin, it is more important than ever to instill in our children a strong foundation of faith and discipline. The discipline we provide now will not only benefit our children in the present, but it will also prepare them for the challenges they will face in the future. Let us embrace the discomfort of discipline with love and patience, knowing that the harvest of righteousness and peace that it produces will be well worth the effort.

So, let us take heart in knowing that the temporary discomfort of discipline is a small price to pay for the long-term benefits it brings. As we continue to nurture our children in the ways of the Lord, let us do so with a spirit of encouragement and love, knowing that we are preparing them to shine brightly in a world that desperately needs the light of Godly children.

Ephesians 6:4 advises, "Fathers, do not exasperate your children; instead, bring them up in the training and instruction of the Lord." This verse balances the need for discipline with the importance of nurturing and instructing our children in a way that does not provoke unnecessary frustration or resentment.

As Christian parents, it is important for us to heed the wise advice found in Ephesians 6:4. This verse reminds us that while discipline is necessary in raising children, it must be balanced with love, nurturing, and instruction in the ways of the Lord. By following this guidance, we can help our children grow into strong, faithful individuals who are equipped to navigate the challenges of the world around them.

Exasperating our children through harsh or unreasonable discipline only serves to breed frustration and resentment. Instead, we are called to approach parenting with a spirit of love and understanding, seeking to build up our children in a way that honors God. By taking the time to listen to our children, understand their unique needs, and guide them with patience and grace, we can create a home environment that fosters growth, respect, and obedience.

Training our children in the ways of the Lord is a vital aspect of nurturing them in a world filled with temptation and sin. By instilling biblical values, teaching them to pray, and encouraging them to seek God in all things, we can help our children develop a strong foundation of faith that will sustain them in times of trial. In doing so, we equip them to make wise choices and stand firm in their beliefs, even when faced with the pressures of an ungodly world.

As Christian parents, we have a responsibility to model the virtues we wish to instill in our children. By living out our faith daily, demonstrating love, forgiveness, and humility, we show our children what it means to walk in the ways of the Lord. This example not only reinforces the lessons we teach them but also strengthens their own commitment to following Christ in a world that often leads them astray.

In conclusion, Ephesians 6:4 offers a powerful reminder of the importance of nurturing our children in a way that reflects the love and wisdom of God. By balancing discipline with love, and instruction with grace, we can raise children who are not only obedient and respectful but who also possess a deep and abiding faith in the Lord. Let us strive to follow this guidance in all aspects of our parenting, trusting in God to guide us as we seek to nurture godly children in an ungodly world.

There will come a time when our children mature and our relationship with them evolves. As they grow older and more independent, the dynamics shift, allowing for a more friendship like relationship. But until that time, our primary responsibility is to be their parent, providing the guidance and boundaries they need to thrive.

As Christian parents, our ultimate goal is to raise our children to be godly individuals who can navigate the challenges of an ungodly world with strength and grace. This journey begins with us being their parents first and foremost, providing the guidance and boundaries they need to thrive. While it may be tempting to want to be their friend, our primary responsibility is to instill in them the values and principles that will guide them throughout their lives.

There will come a time when our children mature and our relationship with them evolves. As they grow older and more independent, the dynamics shift, allowing for a more friendship like relationship. But until that time, it is crucial for us to maintain our role as their parent, offering them the love, support, and discipline they need to flourish.

It can be challenging to find the balance between being a nurturing parent and a disciplinarian, but it is essential for their growth and development. By setting clear boundaries and expectations, we are helping our children understand the difference between right and wrong, and guiding them to- wards making wise choices in a world filled with temptation.

As we navigate the ups and downs of parenthood, it is important to remember that our children are watching and learning from us. Our actions speak louder than words, and by modeling godly behavior and values, we can help shape their character and faith. Let us strive to be the examples they need, showing them what it means to walk in faith and righteousness.

In the end, our goal is to raise children who are grounded in their faith, resilient in the face of temptation, and equipped to make a positive impact on the world around them. By being their parent first and foremost, we are laying the foundation for a strong and enduring relationship that will guide them through life's challenges and triumphs. Let us embrace our role with love, patience, and perseverance, trusting in God to guide us every step of the way.

By adhering to biblical principles and focusing on our role as parents, we help our children develop a sense of security and understanding of right and wrong. In the long run, they will appreciate the love and care behind our actions, even if it means temporarily sacrificing the status of being their "friend."

As Christian parents, it is our responsibility to raise our children in a way that aligns with biblical principles. By doing so, we are not only helping them develop a strong moral compass, but also instilling in them a sense of security and understanding of right and wrong. This foundation will serve as a guiding light for them as they navigate the challenges of the world around them.

It is important to remember that our role as parents is not just to be our children's friends, but to be their guides and mentors. This may mean making decisions that are not always popular with our children in the short term, but are ultimately in their best interest in the long run. By setting boundaries and expectations based on biblical teachings, we are showing our children that we love them enough to prioritize their spiritual and emotional well-being over their temporary happiness.

While it can be difficult to see our children struggle or be upset with us for enforcing rules, we must trust in the greater plan that God has for them. By adhering to biblical principles and focusing on our role as parents, we are sowing seeds of faith and trust in our children that will bear fruit in their lives as they grow and mature.

Our children may not always understand or appreciate the sacrifices we make for them, but in the end, they will come to see the love and care behind our actions. By standing firm in our convictions and leading by example, we are teaching our children valuable lessons that will shape their character and guide them in making wise choices.

In a world filled with temptation and moral ambiguity, it is more important than ever to raise children who are grounded in their faith and values. By nurturing our children in a way that reflects God's love and teachings, we are equipping them to navigate the challenges of an ungodly world with grace and strength. Let us continue to be steadfast in our commitment to raising godly children, even if it means sacrificing the status of being their "friend" in the short term. The rewards of seeing our children grow into mature, faithful adults who understand right from wrong will far outweigh any temporary discomfort or resistance we may encounter along the way.

CHAPTER FOUR

BUILDING BONDS AND SELF-LOVE

*J*n this chapter, we will explore the importance of building strong bonds with our children and teaching them the value of self-love in a world filled with temptation. As Christian parents and adults, it is our duty to nurture our children in a way that prepares them to navigate the challenges of an ungodly world with grace and courage.

One of the first steps in building strong bonds with our children is to prioritize quality time together. In a world filled with distractions and busyness, it can be easy to let our relationships with our children fall by the wayside. However, by setting aside intentional time to connect with our children, we can show them how much we value and love them. Whether it's through shared activities, meaningful conversations, or simply spending time in each other's presence, these moments of connection are essential for building a strong foundation of trust and love.

Additionally, it is crucial to teach our children the importance of self-love in a world that often promotes self-doubt and insecurity. As Christian parents, we must instill in our children the belief that they are fearfully and wonderfully made in the image of God. By helping them develop a healthy sense of self-worth and confidence, we can empower them to resist the pressures of society and stand firm in their identity as beloved children of God.

Furthermore, building strong bonds with our children and teaching them the value of self- love go hand in hand. When our children feel secure in our love and acceptance, they are better equipped to develop a positive self-image and resist negative influences. By modeling self-love and self-respect in our own lives, we can show our children what it means to embrace their unique identity and walk in the truth of who God created them to be.

In conclusion, as Christian parents and adults, we have a sacred responsibility to nurture our children in a way that equips them to thrive in a world filled with temptation. By building strong bonds with our children and teaching them the value of self-love, we can empower them to navigate life with confidence, courage, and grace. Let us commit to investing in our relationships with our children and guiding them on the path of embracing their true identity as beloved children of God.

As parents, it's important to teach our children to love themselves and build strong bonds with their family members. The saying "charity begins at home" means that kindness and love start in the family. When children learn to love and respect themselves, they can better love and respect others.

As parents, it is our responsibility to teach our children the importance of loving themselves and building strong bonds with their family members. In the fast-paced and often chaotic world we live in, it can be easy for children to lose sight of the value of self-love and familial relationships. However, as Christian parents, we must instill in our children the understanding that charity truly does begin at home. By fostering a foundation of love and respect within our families, we are setting our children up for a lifetime of fulfilling relation- ships and a deep sense of self-worth.

When children learn to love and respect themselves, they are better equipped to love and respect others. This is a fundamental principle that we must instill in our children from a young age. By teaching our children to prioritize self-care, self-acceptance, and self- respect, we are helping them develop a strong sense of identity and confidence.

This, in turn, allows them to approach relationships with others from a place of love and understanding, rather than insecurity or fear.

In a world filled with temptation and negativity, it can be challenging for children to navigate their way through relationships and self-acceptance. However, by nurturing a loving and supportive family environment, we are providing our children with a safe haven where they can learn and grow. Encouraging our children to love themselves and build strong bonds with their family members is essential in helping them withstand the pressures and challenges they may face in the world outside of our homes.

As Christian parents, we must lead by example in showing our children what it means to love and respect ourselves and our family members. By demonstrating kindness, compassion, and forgiveness within our own family unit, we are teaching our children valuable lessons that they can carry with them throughout their lives. It is through our actions and words that we can show our children the true meaning of charity beginning at home.

In conclusion, as parents, it is crucial that we prioritize teaching our children to love themselves and build strong bonds with their family members. By instilling in them the values of self-love, respect, and kindness, we are equipping them with the tools they need to navigate the challenges of the world with grace and integrity. Let us continue to nurture our children in a way that reflects the love and grace of God, guiding them on a path of self-discovery and connection with their family members.

The Bible says in Matthew 22:39, "Love your neighbor as yourself." This shows that loving ourselves is important for loving others. Teaching children to take care of themselves helps them feel good and be able to form healthy relationships.

In Matthew 22:39, Jesus teaches us to love our neighbors as ourselves. This powerful statement reminds us that in order to truly love others, we must first learn to love and take care of ourselves. As Christian parents and adults, it is our responsibility to teach our children the importance of self love and self-care. By instilling these values in our children from a young age, we are equipping them to form healthy relationships with others and to spread love and kindness in the world around them.

When we teach children to take care of themselves, we are helping them build a strong foundation for self-esteem and confidence. By encouraging them to practice self-care activities such as eating well, getting enough rest, and engaging in activities that bring them joy, we are showing them that their well-being is important. When children learn to prioritize their own needs and emotions, they are better equipped to empathize with and care for others.

By nurturing a sense of self-love in our children, we are also teaching them to respect and value themselves. When children have a healthy sense of self-worth, they are more likely to set boundaries in relationships and stand up for themselves when necessary. This self- respect translates into how they treat others, as they learn to treat others with the same level of kindness and compassion that they show themselves.

In a world filled with temptation and negative influences, it is more important than ever to teach our children the value of self-love. By helping them cultivate a positive self-image and instilling in them a sense of self-worth, we are empowering them to resist negative peer pressure and make choices that align with their values. When children learn to love and care for themselves, they are better equipped to navigate the challenges of an ungodly world with grace and strength.

As Christian parents and adults, let us lead by example and show our children the importance of loving themselves. By teaching them to prioritize self-care and self-love, we are helping them develop the tools they need to form healthy relationships and spread God's love in the world. Let us nurture our children in a way that empowers them to shine bright in a world that desperately needs their light.

Encouraging children to bond with their siblings and family is also very important. Psalm 133:1 says, "How good and pleasant it is when God's people live together in unity!" When families live in harmony, children feel loved and understood, which helps them develop empathy and cooperation.

Encouraging children to bond with their siblings and family is crucial in fostering a strong foundation of love and unity within the household. As Psalm 133:1 beautifully expresses, there is great goodness and pleasure in God's people living together in harmony. When families prioritize creating a peaceful and loving environment, children are able to thrive and grow in their relationships with one another. This sense of unity not only strengthens the family bond but also teaches children the importance of empathy and cooperation.

In a world filled with temptations and distractions, it is more important than ever for Christian parents to instill in their children the value of family relationships. By encouraging siblings to bond and spend quality time together, parents are fostering a sense of belonging and security within the family unit. This sense of closeness and connection can help children navigate the challenges of the world with confidence and resilience.

When children feel loved and understood within their family, they are more likely to exhibit empathy and compassion towards others. By nurturing strong sibling relationships, parents are teaching their children the importance of caring for and supporting one another. This foundation of empathy and cooperation not only benefits the family dynamic but also extends into other relationships outside the home, helping children to become kind and considerate individuals in a world that often values selfishness and individualism.

As Christian parents, it is our responsibility to raise our children in a way that reflects the teachings of the Bible. By prioritizing family unity and encouraging sibling bonding, we are embodying the values of love, patience, and forgiveness that are central to our faith. In doing so, we are equipping our children with the tools they need to navigate the challenges of the world and remain steadfast in their beliefs.

In conclusion, nurturing strong sibling bonds and fostering family unity is essential in raising godly children in an ungodly world. By following the guidance of Psalm 133:1 and creating a harmonious and loving environment within our families, we are laying a foundation of empathy, cooperation, and faith that will guide our children throughout their lives. Let us continue to prioritize the importance of family relationships and encourage our children to build strong connections with their siblings, knowing that in doing so, we are nurturing their hearts and souls in the ways of the Lord.

Respect is a key part of good relationships. Ephesians 4:32 says, "Be kind and compassionate to one another, forgiving each other, just as in Christ God forgave you." Teaching children to be kind and forgive helps them learn to solve problems and build strong connections.

Respect is a key part of good relationships, and as Christian parents and adults, it is important for us to teach our children the value of treating others with kindness and compassion. Ephesians 4:32 serves as a powerful reminder of this, urging us to be forgiving just as God forgave us through Christ. By instilling these values in our children from a young age, we are helping them develop the skills needed to navigate conflicts and build strong connections with others.

Teaching children to be kind and forgiving is not always easy, but it is an essential aspect of raising godly children in an ungodly world. When we model forgiveness and compassion in our own lives, we are showing our children the importance of these virtues in building healthy relationships. By encouraging our children to be understanding and forgiving towards others, we are helping them cultivate empathy and develop a strong moral compass.

In a world filled with temptation and discord, it is crucial for us to equip our children with the tools they need to navigate the complexities of relationships with grace and integrity. By teaching them to be kind and forgiving, we are empowering them to overcome conflicts and build lasting connections with others. As Christian parents and adults, it is our responsibility to guide our children on the path of righteousness, showing them the way to emulate Christ's love and forgiveness in their interactions with others.

Respect is not just a virtue, but a fundamental building block of good relationships. When we teach our children to be kind and compassionate, we are fostering a culture of respect and understanding that will serve them well throughout their lives. By following the teachings of Ephesians 4:32 and leading by example, we can help our children grow into compassionate and forgiving individuals who are capable of building strong, healthy relationships with others.

In a world that often values self-interest and division, it is more important than ever for us to nurture godly children who will bring light and love into the world. By emphasizing the importance of respect, kindness, and forgiveness in their interactions with others, we are not only shaping the character of our children but also sowing the seeds of a more harmonious and compassionate society. Let us continue to guide our children with love and wisdom, helping them be- come beacons of God's grace in a world that sorely needs it.

Helping each other is another way to build bonds. Galatians 6:2 says, "Carry each other's burdens, and in this way you will fulfill the law of Christ." When children help and support each other, they learn responsibility and empathy, which are important for forming good relationships outside the home.

In the journey of raising children in a world filled with temptations, it is important for Christian parents and adults to instill in them the value of helping each other. Galatians 6:2 reminds us of the importance of carrying each other's bur- dens, just as Christ did for us. By encouraging our children to support and assist their peers, we are not only teaching them responsibility but also fostering empathy and compassion.

When children learn to help and support each other, they are developing essential skills that will serve them well in forming strong relationships outside the home. By actively engaging in acts of kindness and service towards their peers, children are not only fulfilling the law of Christ but also building bonds that will last a lifetime. As parents and adults, it is our responsibility to guide and encourage our children in this journey of nurturing godly relationships.

Teaching children to carry each other's burdens is a powerful way to show them the love and grace of Christ. By modeling this behavior ourselves and encouraging our children to do the same, we are equipping them with the tools they need to navigate the challenges of an ungodly world. Through acts of kindness and service, children can experience the joy and fulfillment that comes from helping others in need.

As Christian parents and adults, we have the privilege and responsibility to nurture godly children in a world filled with temptation. By teaching our children to carry each other's burdens, we are not only instilling in them the values of responsibility and empathy but also helping them to fulfill the law of Christ. Let us continue to guide and support our children in building strong relationships based on love, kindness, and compassion.

In conclusion, helping each other is another way to build bonds that are rooted in Christ's love. As we encourage our children to support and assist their peers, we are empowering them to fulfill the law of Christ and navigate the challenges of an ungodly world. Let us continue to nurture godly children who understand the importance of carrying each other's burdens and who are equipped to build lasting relationships based on love and compassion.

Parents can teach these values through daily interactions and intentional lessons. Encourage children to share their feelings, listen to each other, and work together on family projects. Create chances for them to help one another, whether it's with chores, schoolwork, or personal challenges.

As Christian parents navigating the challenges of raising children in an increasingly ungodly world, it is essential for us to instill important values in our children from a young age. One of the most effective ways to do this is through daily interactions and intentional lessons. By encouraging our children to share their feelings, listen to each other, and work together on family projects, we can help them develop important virtues such as empathy, communication, and teamwork.

Creating opportunities for our children to help one another is another powerful way to teach them valuable lessons. Whether it's dividing up chores around the house, assisting each other with schoolwork, or supporting each other through personal challenges, we can show our children the importance of selflessness, compassion, and unity. By modeling these behaviors ourselves and fostering a spirit of cooperation within our families, we can help our children learn to prioritize the needs of others and work together towards common goals.

Through intentional lessons and daily interactions, we can also teach our children the importance of faith and trust in God. By incorporating prayer, scripture reading, and discussions about God's love and guidance into our daily routines, we can help our children develop a strong foundation of faith that will sustain them in the face of temptation and challenges. By encouraging our children to lean on God for strength and wisdom, we can instill in them the values of faith, resilience, and reliance on God's power.

As Christian parents, it is our responsibility to nurture our children's spiritual growth and character development in a world that often promotes values contrary to those of our faith. By intentionally teaching our children important virtues such as empathy, communication, and teamwork through daily interactions and intentional lessons, we can help them navigate the challenges of an ungodly world with grace and integrity. Let us strive to create a loving and supportive environment where our children can learn to help one another, trust in God, and live out their faith in a way that honors Him.

By teaching self-love, respect, and mutual support, parents help their children become kind and loving people. As they grow, these values will guide them in their interactions with others, fulfilling the Bible's call to love and care for one another.

In a world that often promotes selfishness and individualism, it is crucial for Christian parents to instill in their children the values of self-love, respect, and mutual support. By teaching these principles from a young age, parents can help their children become kind and loving individuals who embody the teachings of the Bible. As children grow and develop, these values will serve as a compass, guiding them in their interactions with others and fulfilling the Bible's call to love and care for one another.

Self-love is not about being self-centered or egotistical, but rather about understanding and accepting oneself as a child of God. When children learn to love themselves, they are better equipped to show love and compassion to others. By teaching children to respect themselves and their worth as individuals, parents can help them navigate the challenges of life with confidence and grace.

Mutual support is another crucial value that parents can teach their children. By encouraging children to support and lift up their peers, parents are fostering a sense of community and unity among young people. This spirit of mutual support will guide children in their interactions with others, helping them to build strong and meaningful relationships based on love and respect.

As Christian parents, it is our responsibility to nurture our children in a world that often promotes values that are contrary to those found in the Bible. By teaching our children self love, respect, and mutual support, we are equipping them with the tools they need to navigate the challenges of life with grace and compassion. These values will not only help our children become kind and loving individuals, but will also fulfill the Bible's call to love and care for one an- other.

Let us strive to raise children who embody the teachings of the Bible, who show love and compassion to all those they encounter, and who uphold the values of self-love, respect, and mutual support. By doing so, we are not only nurturing godly children in an ungodly world, but we are also creating a brighter and more loving future for all.

CHAPTER FIVE

BE A GOOD EXAMPLE

*a*s Christian parents and adults, it is essential for us to be a shining example of God's love and grace to our children. In a world filled with temptation and sin, our actions speak louder than words. Our children are always watching and learning from us, so it is crucial that we model the values and principles of the Bible in everything we do.

One way to be a good example to our children is to prioritize our relationship with God. By spending time in prayer, reading the Bible, and attending church regularly, we show our children the importance of a personal relationship with God. When our children see us seeking God's guidance and wisdom in all aspects of our lives, they will be more likely to do the same.

Another important aspect of being a good example is demonstrating love and forgiveness towards others. As Christians, we are called to love our neighbors as ourselves and to forgive those who have wronged us. By showing kindness and compassion to others, we teach our children the importance of treating others with respect and understanding.

It is also crucial for us to demonstrate integrity and honesty in our actions. Our children should see us being truthful and trustworthy in all situations, even when it is difficult. By modeling these values, we instill in our children the importance of being people of character and integrity.

In conclusion, being a good example to our children is an ongoing process that requires intentionality and effort. By prioritizing our relationship with God, demonstrating love and forgiveness towards others, and showing integrity and honesty in our actions, we can nurture godly children in an ungodly world. Let us strive to be the light of Christ to our children and lead them on a path of righteousness and faith.

Parents, what we do matters more than what we say. Our kids learn from watching us. One day, I was arguing with my wife, and I saw my daughter watching us closely. I quickly changed the mood to something positive.

Parents, what we do matters more than what we say. Our kids learn from watching us. As Christian parents, it is crucial that we model godly behavior and values for our children to follow. One day, I was arguing with my wife, and I saw my daughter watching us closely. In that moment, I realized the impact our actions have on our children's perception of what it means to be a follower of Christ. I quickly changed the mood to something positive, showing my daughter the importance of resolving conflict in a loving and respectful manner.

Our children are like sponges, absorbing everything they see and hear. It is our responsibility as parents to provide them with a strong foundation in faith and morality. By demonstrating godly behavior in our daily lives, we teach our children the importance of living according to God's word. When we prioritize our relationship with God and strive to be examples of His love and grace, our children will be more likely to embrace these values as they navigate the challenges of the world around them.

As parents, we must be mindful of the impact our words and actions have on our children's spiritual development. It is easy to get caught up in the busyness of life and forget the importance of being intentional in our parenting. However, we must remember that our children are always watching and learning from us, even when we least expect it. By prioritizing our own relationship with God and striving to live out our faith in tangible ways, we can help our children grow into strong, faithful followers of Christ.

In a world filled with temptation and moral relativism, it is more important than ever for Christian parents to be diligent in nurturing godly children. Our children face countless challenges and influences that can lead them astray from their faith. By taking the time to invest in their spiritual growth and leading by example, we can equip them with the tools they need to withstand the pressures of the world and stand firm in their beliefs.

Let us remember that our actions speak louder than words. By living out our faith in a visible and authentic way, we can inspire our children to do the same. Let us strive to be the kind of parents who not only talk the talk but walk the walk, showing our children what it truly means to follow Christ in a world that desperately needs His light. Together, we can raise up a generation of godly children who will impact the world for Christ.

The Bible says in Proverbs 22:6, "Teach children how they should live, and they will remember it all their lives." Our actions shape our kids' future. When we are kind and patient, they learn to be the same.

As Christian parents and adults, we are called to nurture our children in the ways of the Lord, even in a world filled with temptation and challenges. The Bible reminds us in Proverbs 22:6 that it is our responsibility to teach our children how they should live, so that they may carry these lessons with them throughout their lives. Our actions play a crucial role in shaping our kids' future, and it is through our kindness and patience that they learn to emulate these virtues.

It can be easy to feel overwhelmed by the pressures and dis- tractions of the world around us, but we must remember that our children are always watching and learning from us. By modeling godly behavior and instilling biblical values in our daily interactions with them, we are setting a firm foundation for them to build upon. Whether it is showing forgiveness, practicing humility, or demonstrating compassion, our actions have a lasting impact on our children's character development.

In a society that often glorifies material wealth, instant gratification, and self-centeredness, it is more important than ever to raise children who prioritize faith, integrity, and serving others. By prioritizing these values in our own lives and passing them on to our children, we are equipping them to navigate the challenges of the world with a strong moral compass. Just as a tree grows with strong roots, so too will our children flourish when grounded in the teachings of the Bible.

Let us not grow weary in our efforts to nurture godly children in an ungodly world. Remember that each small act of kindness, each moment of patience, and each lesson in love is planting seeds that will bear fruit in the future. Trust in the power of God to guide us as we raise the next generation of faithful believers, and may we find encouragement in the knowledge that our efforts are not in vain. Together, let us continue to shape our children's hearts and minds with the love and wisdom of the Lord, knowing that our labor is not in vain in the eyes of the Lord.

Ephesians 6:4 tells fathers, "Don't make your children angry but teach them to obey and love the Lord." We should guide our children with love, not anger.

As Christian parents, we are called to raise our children in a way that honors God. Ephesians 6:4 reminds us of the importance of guiding our children with love, rather than anger. It is easy to become frustrated and upset when our children disobey or make mistakes, but we must remember to approach them with a heart of love and understanding.

When we discipline our children out of anger, we run the risk of pushing them away from us and from the Lord. In- stead, we should strive to teach them to obey and love the Lord through gentle guidance and unconditional love.

110

By modeling the love of Christ in our interactions with our children, we can help them develop a deep and lasting relation- ship with God.

It is important to remember that our children are watching and learning from us every day. The way we handle difficult situations and conflicts will shape their understanding of how to respond to challenges in life. By approaching discipline with love and patience, we can show our children the true nature of God's love and forgiveness.

As we strive to nurture godly children in an ungodly world, let us remember the words of Ephesians 6:4. Let us guide our children with love, patience, and understanding, teaching them to obey and love the Lord with all their hearts. By leading with love, we can help our children grow into strong and faithful followers of Christ equipped to navigate the temptations of this world with grace and dignity.

In tough times, it's important to stay calm and listen. James 1:19 says, "Be quick to listen, slow to speak, and slow to get angry." This helps us handle problems peacefully.

In tough times, it's important for us as Christian parents and adults to remember the wise words found in James 1:19, "Be quick to listen, slow to speak, and slow to get angry." This simple yet powerful advice can help us navigate through challenging situations with grace and wisdom. By staying calm and listening attentively, we can effectively address conflicts and problems in a peaceful manner.

As we strive to nurture godly children in an ungodly world, it is crucial for us to model patience and understanding in all circumstances. When our children see us responding with a calm and composed demeanor, they are more likely to emulate this behavior in their own lives. By practicing active listening and showing empathy towards others, we can teach our children valuable lessons in emotional intelligence and conflict resolution.

In the midst of chaos and uncertainty, it can be easy to react impulsively and with anger. However, by following the advice of James 1:19, we can learn to pause, reflect and respond in a more measured way. This not only benefits our own well-being but also sets a positive example for our children on how to handle difficult situations with grace and composure.

By prioritizing listening over speaking and avoiding quick outbursts of anger, we create a peaceful and harmonious environment within our homes. This paves the way for open communication, mutual respect, and stronger relationships with our children. As we strive to raise godly children in an ungodly world, let us remember the importance of staying calm and listening intently, just as God intended for us.

In conclusion, as Christian parents and adults, let us embrace the wisdom of James 1:19 and strive to be quick to listen, slow to speak, and slow to get angry. By practicing these principles in our daily lives, we can create a nurturing and godly environment for our children to thrive in. Let us lead by example and show our children the power of patience, understanding, and peaceful conflict resolution.

When kids see us solving problems without fighting, they learn to do the same. They understand that it's okay to disagree, but it's important to be kind.

In our journey of nurturing godly children in an ungodly world, one of the most important lessons we can teach our children is how to solve problems without resorting to fighting. As Christian parents and adults, it is our responsibility to model healthy conflict resolution for our children. When kids see us handling disagreements with grace and kindness, they learn valuable lessons that will serve them well throughout their lives.

It is natural for disagreements to arise in any relationship, whether it be between siblings, friends, or even parents and children. However, how we handle these disagreements can make all the difference. By showing our children that it is possible to disagree without being unkind or hurtful, we are teaching them important skills that will help them navigate relationships in a positive way.

When children witness adults resolving conflicts peacefully and respectfully, they learn that it is okay to have differing opinions, but it is crucial to treat others with kindness and empathy. This sets a powerful example for our children to follow, showing them that they can express their thoughts and feelings in a respectful manner without resorting to aggression or hostility.

By demonstrating to our children that it is possible to work through disagreements without fighting, we are instilling important values of compassion, understanding, and forgiveness. These are qualities that are essential in building strong, healthy relationships with others. As Christian parents and adults, it is our duty to guide our children in the ways of love and peacemaking, showing them that conflict resolution can be done in a way that honors God.

In conclusion, when kids see us solving problems without fighting, they are learning valuable lessons that will shape their character and behavior for years to come. By modeling kindness, respect, and patience in our own interactions, we are equipping our children with the tools they need to navigate the challenges of an ungodly world with grace and integrity. Let us continue to be shining examples of Christ's love in all that we do, guiding our children towards a life of faith, peace, and harmony.

And when we mess up, it's important to say sorry and make things right. Colossians 3:13 says, "Be patient with each other and forgive others. If someone does wrong to you, forgive that person because the Lord forgave you." Forgiving teaches our kids the power of healing and fixing things.

In the journey of parenting, we all make mistakes. Sometimes we lose our temper, say things we regret, or act in a way that we know is not reflective of our values as Christian parents. But when we mess up, it's important to acknowledge our faults, apologize, and make things right. Colossians 3:13 reminds us to be patient with each other and forgive others, just as the Lord forgave us. By modeling forgiveness to our children, we teach them the power of healing and the importance of fixing things when we make mistakes.

Saying sorry is not always easy, but it is a crucial step in the process of healing and reconciliation. When we apologize to our children for our wrongdoing, we show them that we are willing to take responsibility for our actions and make amends. This humble act of apologizing can strengthen our relationship with our children and teach them the value of humility and self-awareness.

Forgiveness is a powerful tool that can bring about healing and restoration in relationships. When we forgive others, we release ourselves from the burden of anger and resentment, and we open the door to reconciliation and peace. By forgiving those who have wronged us, we demonstrate to our children the transformative power of forgiveness and the importance of extending grace to others.

As Christian parents, it is our responsibility to instill in our children the values of forgiveness, compassion, and empathy. By teaching our children to forgive others, we help them cultivate a heart of love and understanding. When our children see us apologizing and forgiving others, they learn by example and are more likely to emulate these behaviors in their own relationships.

Let us strive to create a home environment where forgiveness, grace, and reconciliation are valued and practiced. By saying sorry and making things right when we mess up, we not only model godly behavior to our children but also create a foundation of love and understanding that will guide them through life's challenges. Remember, forgiveness is not a sign of weakness, but a testament to the strength and grace of God working in our lives.

Remember, our kids copy what we do. If we want them to be kind and loving, we have to show them how by being good examples ourselves.

As parents, it is important to remember that our children look up to us and model their behavior after ours. If we want them to grow up to be kind and loving individuals, we must lead by example and show them how to live a life of goodness and compassion. Our actions speak louder than words, and our children are always watching and learning from us.

In a world filled with temptations and distractions, it can be challenging to raise children who embody the values of love and kindness. However, as Christian parents, it is our responsibility to instill these virtues in our children by demonstrating them in our own lives. By showing them how to treat others with respect and compassion, we can help them develop a strong foundation of moral character.

One of the most effective ways to teach our children about kindness and love is to actively practice these virtues in our daily interactions with others. Whether it is through small acts of kindness, such as helping a neighbor in need or showing empathy towards those who are struggling, we can demonstrate to our children the importance of putting others before ourselves. By making a conscious effort to be kind and loving in all that we do, we can set a positive example for our children to follow.

It is also important to remember that our children are always watching us, even when we are not aware of it. They observe how we respond to challenges and adversity, how we treat others, and how we handle difficult situations. By being mindful of our actions and always striving to be the best version of ourselves, we can show our children the power of love and kindness in action.

In conclusion, as Christian parents, it is our duty to nurture and guide our children in the ways of Godly living. By setting a positive example of kindness and love, we can help our children navigate the challenges of an ungodly world and grow into compassionate and loving individuals. Remember, our kids copy what we do, so let us lead by example and show them the way to a life filled with love, kindness, and faith.

CHAPTER SIX

CREATING A GOD-CENTERED HOME

*a*s Christian parents, it is our ultimate responsibility to create a home environment that is centered on God

and His teachings. In a world filled with temptation and dis- tractions, it can be challenging to instill values and beliefs that are in line with our faith. However, by intentionally focusing on creating a God-centered home, we can provide a solid foundation for our children to navigate the challenges of the world.

One of the key ways to create a God-centered home is through regular family prayer and worship. Setting aside time each day to pray together as a family not only strengthens our connection with God but also reinforces the importance of faith in our daily lives.

Additionally, participating in worship services as a family can deepen our understanding of God's Word and strengthen our bond with one another.

Another vital aspect of creating a God-centered home is modeling Christ like behavior in our interactions with our children and others. Our actions speak louder than words, and our children are constantly watching and learning from us. By demonstrating love, kindness, patience, and forgiveness in our daily interactions, we show our children what it means to live out our faith in a tangible way.

Creating a God-centered home also involves intentionally incorporating God's Word into our daily lives. Reading and discussing Scripture together as a family can provide valuable opportunities for teaching and learning about God's plan for our lives. Additionally, engaging in meaningful conversations about faith and spirituality can help our children develop a deeper understanding of their beliefs and values.

In conclusion, creating a God-centered home is a continuous process that requires intentionality, commitment, and dedication. By prioritizing prayer, worship, modeling

Christ like behavior, and incorporating God's Word into our daily lives, we can nurture godly children in an ungodly world. Let us remain steadfast in our faith and trust in God's guidance as we strive to create a home that glorifies Him in all that we do.

Making your home centered on God means bringing faith into your everyday life. It's about surrounding your children with God's love and teachings in a way that feels natural and loving. Here's how you can do it.

Making your home centered on God means bringing faith into your everyday life. It's about creating an environment where your children are surrounded by God's love and teachings in a way that feels natural and loving. As Christian parents, it is our responsibility to instill the values and beliefs of our faith in our children from a young age. By integrating God into every aspect of our daily routines, we can help our children grow in their relationship with Him and navigate the challenges of living in a world filled with temptation.

One way to make your home centered on God is to start each day with prayer and scripture reading as a family. This sets a positive and spiritual tone for the day ahead, reminding everyone of the importance of putting God first in their lives. Encourage your children to pray for guidance, strength, and wisdom as they go about their day, and discuss how they can apply the teachings of the Bible to their everyday actions and decisions.

Another way to bring faith into your everyday life is to incorporate Christian values into your family's interactions and discussions. Encourage kindness, forgiveness, and compassion towards others, and model these behaviors yourself. Use real life examples to illustrate how these values align with the teachings of Jesus, and help your children understand how they can live out their faith in practical ways.

Creating a home environment that is centered on God also means prioritizing regular attendance at church and involvement in Christian community activities. This allows your children to see the importance of worshiping together with other believers and serving those in need. By actively participating in church events and volunteering opportunities, you can show your children how to live out their faith in a tangible and meaningful way.

In summary, making your home centered on God is about more than just attending church on Sundays. It's about infusing your daily routines with the love and teachings of God, and creating an environment where faith is a natural and integral part of your family life. By nurturing your children in a way that aligns with your Christian beliefs, you can help them grow into Godly individuals who are equipped to navigate the challenges of an ungodly world with grace and strength.

Praying Together

Praying together as a family is a powerful way to nurture godly children in a world filled with temptation. When we come together in prayer, we invite God into our homes and hearts, creating a sense of unity and strength that can help us navigate the challenges of the world around us. As Christian parents and adults, it is our responsibility to lead by example and show our children the importance of turning to God in times of need.

One of the most beautiful aspects of praying together as a family is the opportunity to share our hopes, fears, and struggles with one another. By opening up to each other in prayer, we create a safe space for our children to express themselves and seek support from their loved ones. This practice can help strengthen family bonds and encourage open communication, fostering a sense of trust and understanding among family members.

Additionally, praying together allows us to teach our children the importance of relying on God for guidance and strength. When we come together in prayer, we demonstrate our faith in God's ability to provide for us and protect us from harm. This can be a powerful lesson for children, helping them to develop a strong foundation of faith that will carry them through life's challenges.

Furthermore, praying together as a family can be a source of comfort and reassurance in times of uncertainty. When we face difficult situations or feel overwhelmed by the pressures of the world, coming together in prayer can provide a sense of peace and calm that can help us navigate through the storm. By turning to God in prayer, we can find the strength and courage to face whatever obstacles come our way.

In conclusion, praying together as a family is a valuable tool for nurturing godly children in an ungodly world. By coming together in prayer, we can create a sense of unity and strength that can help us navigate the challenges of the world around us. Let us continue to lead by example and show our children the importance of turning to God in times of need, so that they may grow in their faith and walk confidently in the path that God has set before them.

Praying together as a family is a powerful way to feel close to God. Make it a habit to pray before meals, at bedtime, and during family times. Encourage your children to talk to God about anything whether they're happy, sad, scared, or thankful.

Praying together as a family is a powerful way to feel close to God. It creates a sense of unity and strength within the family unit, and it allows each member to connect with

God in a personal way. Make it a habit to pray before meals, at bedtime, and during family times.

By incorporating prayer into your daily routine, you are teaching your children the importance of seeking God in all aspects of life. Encourage your children to talk to God about anything whether they're happy, sad, scared, or thankful. Remind them that God is always there to listen and provide comfort and guidance.

When you pray together as a family, you are setting a positive example for your children. They will see the importance of seeking God in times of need and giving thanks for His blessings. By making prayer a regular part of your family life, you are instilling in your children a strong foundation of faith that will guide them throughout their lives. Encourage your children to share their thoughts and feelings with God, knowing that He is always there to listen and provide comfort.

Prayer is a powerful tool that can bring your family closer together and strengthen your relationship with God. When you come together as a family to pray, you are creating a sacred space where you can share your joys, sorrows, and fears with one another and with God. Encourage your children to express their thoughts and feelings through prayer, knowing that God is always there to listen and offer guidance. By fostering a culture of prayer within your family, you are nurturing your children in their faith and helping them develop a deep and meaningful relationship with God.

As Christian parents, it is important to lead by example and show your children the importance of prayer in your own life. When they see you turning to God in times of trouble and offering thanks in times of joy, they will learn to do the same. By making prayer a priority in your family, you are creating a spiritual foundation that will support your children as they navigate the challenges of the world. Encourage your children to pray regularly and to seek God's guidance in all aspects of their lives, knowing that He is always there to listen and provide comfort.

In a world filled with temptation and distractions, it is more important than ever to nurture godly children who are grounded in their faith. By making prayer a central part of your family life, you are instilling in your children a strong foundation of faith that will carry them through life's trials and tribulations. Encourage your children to talk to God about anything and everything, knowing that He is always there to listen and provide guidance. Together as a family, you can create a powerful bond with God that will sustain you through all of life's challenges.

You can say simple prayers like, "Thank you, God, for this food and for our family. Help us be kind and loving.

Amen." Or, at bedtime, "Thank you, God, for the fun we had today. Please help us sleep well and have a good day tomorrow."

As Christian parents, it is important to teach our children the value of prayer from a young age. Simple prayers can help instill gratitude, kindness, and love in their hearts. One easy way to incorporate prayer into your daily routine is by saying a prayer before meals.

Encourage your children to join in as you thank God for the food on your table and ask for His guidance in being kind and loving towards one another.

Bedtime prayers are another wonderful opportunity to connect with God as a family. Before tucking your children in at night, take a moment to say a prayer together. Thank God for the fun moments of the day and ask for a restful night's sleep and a good day ahead. This practice not only helps children develop a sense of security and peace before bed but also teaches them the importance of turning to God in times of need.

Remember, it's not about reciting elaborate prayers or using fancy language. What matters most is the sincerity and intention behind the words. Encourage your children to speak from the heart and share their thoughts, feelings, and concerns with God. By keeping prayers simple and relatable, children can learn to cultivate a personal relationship with their Heavenly Father.

In a world filled with distractions and temptations, teaching your children to pray is a powerful way to help them navigate life's challenges. Prayer is a tool that can provide comfort, strength, and guidance in times of uncertainty. By encouraging your children to pray regularly, you are equipping them with a valuable resource that will serve them well throughout their lives.

So, take the time to incorporate simple prayers into your daily routine. Whether it's before meals, at bedtime, or during moments of joy or sadness, let prayer be a constant presence in your home. By nurturing your children's spiritual growth in this way, you are helping them build a strong foundation rooted in faith, love, and trust in God.

Living Out Faith Every Day

Living out faith every day is a crucial aspect of nurturing godly children in a world filled with temptation. As Christian parents and adults, it is our responsibility to model a life of faith and righteousness for our children to follow. This means demonstrating our beliefs not just on Sundays or special occasions, but in our everyday actions and interactions. By living out our faith consistently, we show our children what it means to truly walk with God and inspire them to do the same.

One way to live out faith every day is through prayer. Taking the time to pray with your children and for your children on a daily basis can have a powerful impact on their spiritual growth. By showing them the importance of turning to God in all circumstances, you are teaching them to rely on Him for guidance and strength. Encourage your children to pray for others, for themselves, and for the world around them. By making prayer a regular part of your family's routine, you are instilling in them a deep connection to their faith.

Another way to live out faith every day is by actively seeking opportunities to serve others. Whether it's volunteering at a local shelter, helping a neighbor in need, or simply showing kindness to strangers, demonstrating a servant's heart can make a lasting impression on your children. By showing them the importance of putting others before themselves, you are teaching them to live out the principles of love and compassion that are at the core of the Christian faith.

Living out faith every day also means being intentional about sharing the gospel with your children. Take the time to read the Bible together, discuss its teachings, and answer any questions they may have. By equipping your children with a solid foundation of biblical knowledge, you are preparing them to face the challenges and temptations of the world with a strong and unwavering faith. Encourage them to share their faith with others and to be bold in standing up for what they believe in.

In conclusion, living out faith every day is a powerful way to nurture godly children in an ungodly world. By modeling a life of faith, prayer, service, and sharing the gospel, you are setting an example for your children to follow. Remember that your actions speak louder than words, and by living out your faith consistently, you are shaping the hearts and minds of the next generation. Stay strong, stay faithful, and trust in God to guide you as you raise children who will shine brightly in a world filled with darkness.

Show your children how to live their faith every day through your actions. Be kind, patient, and forgiving. When you help others, explain that you're doing it because it's what God wants us to do.

As Christian parents, it is vital to not only teach our children about our faith, but also to show them how to live it out every day through our actions. Children learn best by example, so it is important to model kindness, patience, and forgive- ness in all that we do. When we exhibit these qualities in our interactions with others, we are demonstrating the love of God in a tangible way.

One of the most powerful ways to teach our children about living out their faith is by helping others. When we reach out to those in need, whether it be through acts of service or simply offering a listening ear, we show our children that this is what God wants us to do. By explaining to them that we are helping others because of our faith, we are instilling in them the importance of living out the values and teachings of Christianity.

It is also important to be intentional about incorporating faith-based activities into our daily lives. Whether it is praying together as a family, reading scripture, or attending church services, these practices help to reinforce the beliefs and values that we are seeking to instill in our children. By making faith a central part of our daily routines, we are helping our children to see the significance of their relationship with God.

Furthermore, it is important to be patient and understanding with our children as they navigate their own faith journey. Encourage them to ask questions, seek out answers, and explore their beliefs. By fostering an environment of open communication and acceptance, we are helping our children to develop a strong foundation of faith that will guide them throughout their lives.

In a world filled with temptation and distractions, it is more important than ever to equip our children with the tools they need to navigate the challenges they will face. By showing them how to live out their faith through our actions, we are giving them a solid foundation to stand on. Let us strive to be examples of kindness, patience, and forgiveness, and to always point our children towards the love and light of God.

Get your children involved in helping others, like sharing food with a neighbor or donating toys to kids in need. Explain that these acts of kindness are ways to show God's love.

As Christian parents, it is important to instill in our children the value of helping others and showing God's love through acts of kindness. One way to do this is by getting our children involved in activities that benefit those in need, such as sharing food with a neighbor or donating toys to kids who are less fortunate. By involving our children in these acts of kindness, we are teaching them the importance of empathy and compassion, and showing them how they can make a positive impact in the world around them.

When we encourage our children to help others, we are not only teaching them to be kind and generous, but we are also showing them how to live out their faith in practical ways. By sharing God's love through acts of service, our children can see firsthand the power of love and how it can transform lives. This hands-on approach to teaching them about God's love will help them to develop a heart for serving others and inspire them to continue to seek out opportunities to make a difference in the world.

Involving our children in acts of kindness also helps to foster a sense of community and connection with those around them. When they see the impact that their actions can have on others, they will develop a greater sense of empathy and understanding for those who are in need. By teaching our children to look beyond themselves and to consider the needs of others, we are helping them to cultivate a spirit of generosity and selflessness that reflects the love of God.

By getting our children involved in helping others, we are not only shaping them into compassionate individuals, but we are also helping them to grow in their faith. As they wit- ness the positive impact of their actions and experience the joy that comes from serving others, they will begin to understand the importance of living out their faith in tangible ways. By encouraging them to share God's love through acts of kindness, we are equipping them to be true Disciples of Christ and to be a light in a world that is in desperate need of hope and love.

So let us continue to encourage our children to get involved in helping others, whether it be through sharing food with a neighbor or donating toys to kids in need. By teaching them to show God's love through acts of kindness, we are not only nurturing them to be godly children in an ungodly world, but we are also helping them to develop a heart for serving others and making a positive impact in the world around them.

Talking About Faith

In a world filled with temptation and distractions, it can of- ten be challenging to raise children who are grounded in their faith. As Christian parents and adults, it is our responsibility to instill in our children a strong foundation of faith that will guide them through life's challenges. One of the most important aspects of nurturing godly children is having open and honest conversations about faith.

Talking about faith with your children may seem daunting at first, but it is essential for their spiritual growth and development. By discussing your own beliefs and experiences with God, you can help your children understand the importance of faith in their lives.

Encourage them to ask questions and engage in meaningful discussions about their own beliefs and values.

It is crucial to lead by example when it comes to talking about faith with your children. Show them through your actions and words what it means to live a life guided by God's love and teachings. Share stories from the Bible and how they have shaped your own beliefs and values. By being authentic and transparent in your conversations about faith, you can inspire your children to develop a deep and meaningful relationship with God.

Create opportunities for your children to explore their faith through prayer, worship, and service. Encourage them to participate in church activities and community service projects that align with their values and beliefs. By actively engaging in spiritual practices, your children will develop a deeper connection with God and a greater sense of purpose in their lives.

Remember, nurturing godly children in an ungodly world is a journey that requires patience, love, and faith. By talking openly and honestly about faith with your children, you are laying the foundation for a lifetime of spiritual growth and fulfillment. Trust in God's guidance and continue to cultivate a nurturing environment where your children can flourish in their relationship with Him.

Make it easy for your children to talk about their faith. Encourage them to ask questions and share their thoughts. Share your own experiences with them, too.

As Christian parents, it is important to create an open and welcoming environment for our children to talk about their faith. Encouraging them to ask questions and share their thoughts will not only strengthen their own understanding of God, but also foster a deeper connection within the family. By actively engaging in conversations about faith, we can help our children navigate the challenges of living in a world filled with temptation.

Sharing our own experiences with our children is a powerful way to demonstrate the relevance of faith in our lives. By opening up about our own struggles and triumphs, we show our children that faith is not just a concept, but a living, breathing part of who we are. This authenticity can inspire our children to do the same, creating a bond of trust and understanding that will carry them through difficult times.

When our children feel comfortable talking about their faith, they are more likely to seek guidance and support when faced with temptations. By fostering a culture of open communication, we empower our children to make informed decisions rooted in their beliefs. This not only strengthens their own faith, but also equips them to be a positive influence in the world around them.

Encouraging our children to ask questions and share their thoughts also allows us to address any doubts or uncertainties they may have. By listening with empathy and providing thoughtful responses, we can help our children deepen their understanding of God and His teachings. This ongoing dialogue is essential for nurturing a strong foundation of faith that will guide our children throughout their lives.

In a world that is constantly bombarding our children with conflicting messages and values, it is more important than ever to create a safe space for them to explore their faith. By making it easy for our children to talk about their beliefs, we can instill in them a sense of confidence and purpose that will help them navigate the challenges of an ungodly world.

Let us continue to encourage our children to ask questions, share their thoughts, and walk alongside them on their journey of faith.

You can have simple conversations about values like honesty or kindness. Talk about what the Bible says and share stories from your own life. For example, discuss why it's important to tell the truth and how Jesus values honesty.

As Christian parents, it is essential to have open and honest conversations with our children about values such as honesty and kindness. These conversations not only help reinforce the importance of these values in their lives, but also provide them with a strong moral foundation to navigate the challenges of an ungodly world. One way to approach these conversations is by turning to the Bible for guidance and sharing stories from our own lives that demonstrate the power of these values.

The Bible is filled with teachings on honesty and integrity, emphasizing the importance of speaking the truth and living a life of integrity. By discussing what the Bible says about these values, we can help our children understand the significance of being honest in their words and actions. For example, we can share stories from the Bible that illustrate how Jesus valued honesty and how his teachings on truthfulness can guide us in our daily lives.

Sharing personal stories with our children can also be a powerful way to reinforce the importance of values like honesty and kindness. By sharing our own experiences of how honesty has played a role in our lives, we can show our children the real life impact of living with integrity. Whether it's admitting to a mistake or speaking up for what is right, our stories can serve as valuable lessons for our children.

It is important to create a safe and open environment for these conversations, where our children feel comfortable sharing their thoughts and experiences. By engaging in discussions about values like honesty and kindness, we can help our children develop a strong moral compass that will guide them in making wise choices in the face of temptation. By fostering a culture of honesty and integrity in our homes, we can empower our children to live out their faith in a world that often challenges their beliefs.

In conclusion, having simple conversations about values like honesty and kindness with our children is crucial in nurturing them to be godly individuals in an ungodly world. By turning to the Bible for guidance, sharing stories from our own lives, and creating a safe space for open dialogue, we can instill in our children the importance of living with integrity and speaking the truth. Let us continue to encourage and support our children in their journey of faith, guiding them with love and wisdom as they navigate the challenges of the world around them.

Celebrating Faith Together

Celebrating faith together is a powerful way to strengthen the bond within your family and instill a deep sense of spirituality in your children. As Christian parents, it is important to create a nurturing and supportive environment where faith can flourish. By celebrating faith together, you are not only reinforcing the values and teachings of the Bible, but you are also creating lasting memories that your children will cherish for years to come.

One of the best ways to celebrate faith together as a family is through regular attendance at church services and events. By participating in worship services, Bible studies, and com- munity outreach programs, you are showing your children the importance of prioritizing their relationship with God. Encourage your children to actively engage in church activities, such as singing in the choir, volunteering in the nursery, or participating in youth group events. This will help them develop a sense of belonging and connection to their faith community.

Another way to celebrate faith together is through prayer and devotionals as a family. Set aside time each day to pray together, read Scripture, and discuss the teachings of the Bible. Encourage your children to share their thoughts, questions, and concerns about their faith journey. By creating a safe and open environment for discussion, you are helping your children deepen their understanding of God's love and teachings.

Celebrating faith together can also involve fun and creative activities that reinforce biblical principles and values. Plan family outings to volunteer at a local charity, organize a family game night centered around Christian values, or create a family scrapbook documenting your spiritual journey together. By incorporating faith into everyday activities, you are making God's presence a central part of your family's life.

In conclusion, celebrating faith together as a family is an essential aspect of nurturing godly children in an ungodly world. By prioritizing your relationship with God and creating a supportive environment for spiritual growth, you are laying a strong foundation for your children's faith journey. Embrace the opportunity to celebrate faith together as a family, and watch as your children develop a deep and lasting connection to their faith that will guide them throughout their lives.

Celebrate religious holidays and special moments together. During Christmas, focus on the story of Jesus' birth. At Easter, talk about Jesus rising from the dead and why it's important.

As Christian parents, it is important to celebrate religious holidays and special moments together with our children. These occasions provide us with the perfect opportunity to instill in them the values and teachings of our faith. During Christmas, it is crucial to focus on the story of Jesus' birth.

Take the time to read the biblical account of the nativity and explain to your children the significance of this miraculous event. Help them understand the true meaning of Christmas and why we celebrate it as believers in Christ.

Similarly, at Easter, it is essential to talk to our children about Jesus rising from the dead and why it is so important to our faith. Share with them the story of the resurrection and dis- cuss the implications of this event for our salvation. Help them grasp the power of Jesus' victory over death and the hope that it brings to all who believe in Him. Use this time to reinforce the truth of the gospel and the transformative impact it has on our lives as Christians.

By celebrating these religious holidays with our children, we are not only creating cherished family traditions but also nurturing their spiritual growth. These moments of reflection and discussion help to strengthen their understanding of the foundational beliefs of our faith. Encourage your children to ask questions and engage in meaningful conversations about the stories and teachings of Jesus. Use these opportunities to deepen their relationship with God and foster a love for His word.

As we navigate the challenges of raising godly children in an ungodly world, let us make the most of these special moments to reinforce the values and principles that we hold dear. Celebrating religious holidays together as a family creates a sense of unity and shared faith that will guide our children as they grow and mature. Let us use these occasions to teach our children the importance of honoring and celebrating the life, death, and resurrection of Jesus Christ. By doing so, we are equipping them to stand firm in their faith and navigate the temptations of the world with a strong foundation in God's truth.

In conclusion, as Christian parents, let us be intentional about celebrating religious holidays and special moments with our children. Use these opportunities to teach them about the stories and teachings of Jesus, and the significance of His birth and resurrection. Encourage open dialogue and foster a love for God's word in your children. By nurturing their spiritual growth in this way, we are equipping them to navigate the challenges of an ungodly world with a firm foundation in their faith. Celebrate these moments together as a family and watch as your children grow in their understanding and love for God.

Get your children involved in these celebrations. Read Bible stories, sing hymns, and go to church together. Making these times special helps your children see how important faith is.

As Christian parents, it is crucial for us to involve our children in the celebration of our faith. One way to do this is by reading Bible stories together. By sharing these stories with our children, we can help them understand the importance of faith and how it can guide them in their lives. Taking the time to discuss these stories with our children can also help them develop a deeper understanding of their faith and how it can shape their values and beliefs.

Another way to involve our children in our faith is by singing hymns together. Music has a powerful way of connecting us to our spirituality and can be a beautiful way to worship together as a family. Encourage your children to participate in singing hymns with you, whether it be at home or in church. This can be a meaningful way to bond as a family and to instill a love for worship in your children.

Attending church together as a family is also an important way to nurture your children's faith. Going to church regularly can help your children see the importance of community and fellowship in their faith journey. Encourage your children to participate in church activities and to build relationships with other members of the congregation. This can help them feel connected to their faith and to the larger Christian community.

Making these times of celebration special can also help your children see how important faith is in their lives. Create traditions around reading Bible stories, singing hymns, and attending church together. This can help your children look forward to these times of worship and reflection, and can create lasting memories that they will carry with them throughout their lives. By making faith a central part of your family life, you can help your children develop a strong foundation of faith that will guide them through the challenges of the world.

In conclusion, involving your children in the celebration of your faith is a powerful way to nurture their spiritual development. By reading Bible stories, singing hymns, and attending church together, you can help your children see the importance of faith in their lives.

Making these times of celebration special can create lasting memories and help your children develop a strong foundation of faith that will guide them through the ups and downs of life. As Christian parents, it is our responsibility to instill a love for God in our children and to help them grow into faithful, Godly individuals.

Daily Reminders of God's Presence

As Christian parents and adults, it is important for us to in still in our children the daily reminders of God's presence in their lives. In a world filled with temptation and distractions, it can be easy for our children to lose sight of God's love and guidance. By consistently reminding them of God's presence, we can help them navigate the challenges they face with faith and courage.

One of the most powerful reminders of God's presence is through prayer. Encouraging our children to pray daily and seek God's guidance in all things helps them develop a personal relationship with Him. By teaching them to turn to God in times of joy and times of need, we show them that God is always with them, ready to listen and provide comfort.

Another daily reminder of God's presence is through scripture. Taking time each day to read and reflect on the Word of God helps our children stay connected to Him and His teachings. By incorporating scripture into our daily routines, we reinforce the importance of God's word in their lives and help them understand the value of living according to His will.

We can also remind our children of God's presence through worship and praise. Encouraging them to participate in church activities, sing hymns, and praise God for His goodness helps them cultivate a heart of gratitude and reverence. By surrounding them with a community of believers who worship and serve God together, we show our children that they are never alone in their faith journey.

In conclusion, as Christian parents and adults, it is our responsibility to nurture our children in the knowledge and love of God. By providing them with daily reminders of God's presence through prayer, scripture, worship, and praise, we equip them with the tools they need to navigate the challenges of this world with faith and strength. Let us continue to encourage and support our children in their spiritual growth, knowing that God is always with them, guiding and protecting them every step of the way.

Find ways to remind your family of God's love every day. This could be through conversations about gratitude and recognizing God's work in your lives. Encourage your children to share moments when they felt God's presence.

As Christian parents, it is important to find ways to remind our families of God's love every day. One simple way to do this is through conversations about gratitude and recognizing God's work in our lives. Encourage your children to share moments when they felt God's presence, whether it be in a beautiful sunset or a kind gesture from a friend. By acknowledging these moments, we are helping our children develop a deeper appreciation for God's love and presence in their lives.

Another way to remind our families of God's love is to incorporate daily prayers and scripture readings into our routines. Taking the time to pray together as a family not only strengthens our bond with each other, but also with God. Reading and discussing scripture together can provide valuable lessons and insights that will help guide our children in their faith journey. By making these practices a priority in our daily lives, we are instilling in our children the importance of seeking God's presence and guidance in all aspects of their lives.

In addition to conversations and prayer, finding ways to actively show God's love to others can also be a powerful re- minder of His presence in our lives. Encourage your family to participate in acts of service and kindness, whether it be volunteering at a local charity or simply helping a neighbor in need. By showing love and compassion to others, we are reflecting God's love in a tangible way and demonstrating to our children the importance of living out their faith in practical ways.

It is also important to create a home environment that fosters a sense of God's love and presence. Displaying scripture verses and Christian art throughout your home can serve as constant reminders of God's love and faithfulness. Creating a peaceful and loving atmosphere in your home can help cultivate a sense of God's presence and provide a safe space for your family to grow in their faith.

In conclusion, finding ways to remind your family of God's love every day is essential in Nurturing Godly Children in an Ungodly World. By engaging in conversations about gratitude, incorporating daily prayers and scripture readings, actively showing God's love to others, and creating a home environment that reflects God's presence, we are helping our children develop a strong foundation of faith that will guide them throughout their lives.

Let us continue to encourage and support one another in raising children who are rooted in God's love and grace.

By doing these things, you make your home a place filled with faith and love. Your children will grow up knowing God's love and learning to live their lives with faith.

By doing these things, you make your home a place filled with faith and love. Your children will grow up knowing God's love and learning to live their lives with faith. One of the most important ways to cultivate a home filled with faith and love is through prayer. Start and end each day with prayer as a family, inviting God into your home and asking for His guidance and protection over your family. Encourage your children to pray for their own needs and the needs of others, fostering a deep connection with God from an early age.

Another way to create a home filled with faith and love is by setting an example of love and kindness. Show your children what it means to love unconditionally, to forgive others, and to serve those in need. By demonstrating these qualities in your own life, you are teaching your children how to live out their faith in practical ways. Remember, actions speak louder than words, so let your love for God shine through in all that you do.

In addition to prayer and setting a loving example, make sure to prioritize time for family devotions and Bible study. Reading and discussing scripture together as a family helps to strengthen your children's faith and deepen their understanding of God's word. It also provides an opportunity for meaningful conversations about faith and encourages your children to ask questions and seek answers.

Furthermore, create a home environment that is filled with positivity and encouragement. Speak words of affirmation and love to your children, building them up and instilling in them a sense of worth and value. Encourage them to pursue their passions and talents, knowing that God has given each of us unique gifts to use for His glory. By creating a safe and nurturing home environment, you are fostering a sense of security and belonging that will help your children grow in their faith and love for God.

In conclusion, by doing these things, you are laying a strong foundation for your children to grow up knowing God's love and living their lives with faith. Your home will become a sanctuary of faith and love, a place where your children can feel safe, loved, and supported as they navigate the challenges of the world. Remember, as Christian parents, you have been entrusted with the precious responsibility of nurturing godly children in an ungodly world. With God's help and guidance, you can create a home that is filled with faith and love, where your children can thrive and grow in their relationship with Him.

CHAPTER SEVEN

THE ROLE THE CHURCH PLAYS

*a*s Christian parents, one of the most important aspects of raising godly children in today's world is the role that the church plays in their upbringing. The church is not just a building where we go to worship on Sundays, but rather a community of believers who come together to support and encourage one another in their faith journey. By actively participating in church activities, children are able to develop a strong foundation of faith that will guide them throughout their lives.

One of the key ways that the church can impact our children is through the teaching and preaching of God's Word. By exposing our children to the teachings of Scripture, they are able to learn about God's love, grace, and plan for their lives. Through Sunday school classes, youth groups, and sermons, children are able to grow in their understanding of the Bible and develop a personal relationship with Jesus Christ.

Additionally, the church provides a sense of community and belonging for our children. By participating in church events and activities, children are able to build relationships with other believers who can serve as positive role models and mentors. These relationships can be instrumental in helping our children navigate the challenges and temptations they may face in the world.

Furthermore, the church offers opportunities for our children to serve others and live out their faith in practical ways. By participating in service projects, mission trips, and out reach programs, children are able to put their faith into action and make a positive impact on the world around them. These experiences help children develop a heart for serving others and instill in them a sense of responsibility to be the hands and feet of Jesus in their communities.

In conclusion, the role that the church plays in nurturing godly children in an ungodly world cannot be overstated. By actively engaging with the church community, our children are able to grow in their faith, build relationships with other believers, and serve others in Jesus' name. As parents, let us encourage our children to be active participants in the life of the church so that they may continue to grow and thrive in their relationship with God.

The church plays a vital role in raising godly children. It serves as a community of believers who support and reinforce the values and teachings you instill at home. Here's how the church can aid in your parenting journey.

As Christian parents, it is our responsibility to raise our children in the ways of the Lord and instill in them godly values and teachings. However, we cannot do this alone. The church plays a vital role in supporting and reinforcing the values we teach at home. It serves as a community of believers who come alongside us in our parenting journey, providing guidance, encouragement, and accountability.

One way the church can aid in our parenting journey is through the teaching and preaching of God's Word. By attending church regularly, our children are exposed to the truths of Scripture and learn about the character of God. This solid foundation helps them navigate the challenges of the world and resist temptation. The church also provides opportunities for children to participate in age appropriate activities, such as Sunday school and youth group, where they can learn and grow in their faith.

Another way the church supports parents in raising godly children is through the example set by other believers. When our children see adults living out their faith, it reinforces the values we are trying to instill at home. The church community can also provide mentorship and guidance to both parents and children, helping them navigate difficult situations and make wise choices. By surrounding ourselves with other believers, we create a network of support that strengthens our family's commitment to following Christ.

In addition to teaching and example-setting, the church can also provide a sense of belonging and community for our children. When they see that they are part of something larger than themselves, it helps them develop a sense of identity and purpose. This sense of belonging can also protect them from the negative influences of the world, as they find acceptance and support within the church family.

In conclusion, the church plays a vital role in raising godly children in a world of temptation. By partnering with the church community, we can provide our children with the spiritual foundation and support they need to navigate the challenges of the world. Let us embrace the community of believers around us and allow them to aid us in our parenting journey, knowing that we do not walk this path alone.

Spiritual Growth and Learning

In the journey of nurturing godly children in an ungodly world, one of the most important aspects to focus on is spiritual growth and learning. As Christian parents and adults, it is crucial to instill in our children a strong foundation of faith and a desire to continually seek a deeper relationship with God. This subchapter will explore the significance of spiritual growth and learning in the lives of our children and provide practical tips on how to cultivate this aspect in their upbringing.

Spiritual growth is a lifelong process that involves developing a deeper understanding of God's word, building a personal relationship with Him, and growing in faith and character. As parents, we have the privilege and responsibility to guide our children in their spiritual journey, helping them to grow in wisdom and maturity. By creating a nurturing and supportive environment that encourages spiritual growth and learning, we can equip our children to navigate the challenges of an ungodly world with grace and strength.

One of the key ways to foster spiritual growth in our children is through regular prayer and scripture study. Encourage your children to develop a habit of daily prayer and reading the Bible, helping them to build a strong foundation of faith. Engage in meaningful conversations about scripture and God's teachings, allowing your children to ask questions and explore their beliefs. By actively participating in their spiritual growth and learning, you can help them to develop a deeper understanding of their faith and cultivate a personal relationship with God.

In addition to prayer and scripture study, it is important to model a life of faith and integrity for your children to emulate. Show them what it means to live out your beliefs in your daily life, demonstrating compassion, forgiveness, and love towards others. By embodying the values of your faith and being a positive role model, you can inspire your children to follow in your footsteps and grow in their own spiritual journey. Remember, your actions speak louder than words, and your children will learn more from how you live your life than what you say.

As you guide your children in their spiritual growth and learning, remember to be patient, encouraging, and supportive. Every child's journey is unique, and it is important to al- low them the space to explore and develop their faith at their own pace. Celebrate their milestones and achievements, and offer words of affirmation and encouragement along the way. By nurturing their spiritual growth with love and compassion, you can help your children to flourish into strong, faithful individuals who will shine brightly in a world filled with temptation and darkness.

The church provides opportunities for children to learn about God and grow in their faith. Sunday school classes, youth groups, and Bible studies offer age appropriate teachings that help children understand and apply biblical principles.

Sunday School: Engaging lessons and activities help children grasp biblical stories and concepts in a way that resonates with them.

As Christian parents and adults in today's world, it can be challenging to raise children who have a strong foundation in their faith. With so many distractions and temptations surrounding them, it is important to provide our children with engaging lessons and activities that will help them grasp biblical stories and concepts in a way that resonates with them. One of the best places to do this is in Sunday School.

Sunday School is a wonderful opportunity for children to learn about the Bible in a fun and interactive way. By engaging with stories and concepts through activities such as arts and crafts, games, and music, children are able to connect with the material on a deeper level. These hands-on experiences help them to remember the lessons they have learned and apply them to their daily lives.

In Sunday School, children are also able to build relationships with their peers and teachers, creating a sense of community and support that can be invaluable as they navigate the challenges of growing up in an ungodly world. By surrounding themselves with like- minded individuals who share their values and beliefs, children are more likely to stay true to their faith and resist temptation.

Furthermore, Sunday School provides children with a safe and nurturing environment where they can ask questions, express their doubts, and explore their faith in a non- judgmental setting. This open dialogue encourages children to think critically about their beliefs and deepen their understanding of the Bible.

By investing time and effort into providing engaging lessons and activities in Sunday School, we are helping our children to develop a strong spiritual foundation that will guide them throughout their lives. As Christian parents and adults, let us continue to support and encourage our children in their faith journey, knowing that the lessons they learn in Sunday School will stay with them long after they have left the classroom.

Youth Groups: These groups provide a space for older children and teenagers to explore their faith, ask questions, and develop a personal relationship with God.

Youth groups play a crucial role in the spiritual development of older children and teenagers. These groups provide a safe and welcoming space for young people to explore their faith, ask questions, and develop a personal relationship with God. As Christian parents and adults, it is important for us to encourage our children to participate in these youth groups, as they can have a profound impact on their spiritual growth.

In a world filled with so many distractions and temptations, youth groups offer a respite where young people can focus on their relationship with God. By engaging in discussions, Bible studies, and prayer sessions with their peers, children and teenagers can deepen their understanding of their faith and learn how to apply it to their daily lives. This can help them navigate the challenges and temptations they may face in the world outside of the youth group.

Youth groups also provide a sense of community and belonging for young people. By participating in group activities, service projects, and social events, children and teenagers can build strong relationships with their peers and adult mentors who share their faith. These connections can provide much needed support and encouragement as they navigate the ups and downs of adolescence.

As Christian parents and adults, we can support our children's involvement in youth groups by encouraging them to participate actively and by being involved ourselves. By attending youth group meetings, volunteering as leaders or mentors, and engaging in discussions with our children about their faith journey, we can show them that we value and support their spiritual growth. This can help strengthen their commitment to their faith and provide them with the foundation they need to resist temptation and stand strong in their beliefs.

In a world that often challenges and tests our children's faith, youth groups can serve as a powerful tool for nurturing godly children in an ungodly world. By providing a space for older children and teenagers to explore their faith, ask questions, and develop a personal relationship with God, these groups can help our children grow into strong and confident Christian adults who are able to withstand the temptations of the world around them. Let us continue to support and encourage our children's involvement in youth groups, knowing that they are essential for raising godly children in today's society.

Community and Fellowship

In the journey of raising our children to be godly in a world filled with temptation, it is crucial to understand the importance of community and fellowship. As Christian parents, we cannot do it alone. We need the support and encouragement of other like-minded individuals who share our values and beliefs. By surrounding ourselves and our children with a strong community of fellow believers, we can provide a foundation of love, support, and accountability that will help guide them in their faith journey.

Community and fellowship play a vital role in nurturing godly children in an ungodly world. When our children see us actively participating in a community of believers, they learn the importance of building relationships with others who share their faith. This sense of belonging and connection to a larger community can help strengthen their faith and provide them with a support system to lean on during times of temptation or struggle.

As Christian parents, it is important for us to model the value of community and fellowship to our children. By actively participating in church activities, small groups, and other community events, we show our children the importance of building relationships with other believers. We also demonstrate the importance of accountability and support in our own lives, which can serve as a powerful example for our children to follow.

In a world that often promotes individualism and self-reliance, it is essential for us as Christian parents to emphasize the value of community and fellowship to our children. By encouraging them to build strong relationships with other believers, we help them develop a sense of belonging and connection that can strengthen their faith and provide them with the support they need to resist temptation and stand firm in their beliefs.

Let us continue to cultivate a strong sense of community and fellowship within our families and churches, knowing that we are not alone in the journey of raising godly children in an ungodly world. Together, we can provide a foundation of love, support, and accountability that will help guide our children in their faith journey and empower them to live out their beliefs in a world filled with temptation.

Being part of a church community allows your children to form meaningful relationships with other believers. This sense of belonging reinforces their faith and provides positive role models.

Church Events: Participating in church events and activities helps children feel connected to their faith community.

As Christian parents and adults, we understand the importance of nurturing our children in the ways of the

Lord. One powerful way to instill and deepen their faith is by encouraging them to participate in church events and activities. These gatherings not only provide a sense of community and belonging but also help children feel connected to their faith community.

Attending church events allows children to witness firsthand the love and support of their fellow believers. Whether it's a youth group outing, a community service project, or a holiday celebration, these events create opportunities for children to bond with others who share their beliefs. This sense of camaraderie can be instrumental in helping children navigate the challenges of growing up in an increasingly secular world.

Furthermore, participating in church events exposes children to a variety of spiritual teachings and practices. From Sunday school lessons to worship services to prayer meetings, these activities provide a rich tapestry of experiences that can help children deepen their understanding of the Bible and their relationship with God. By immersing themselves in these events, children can develop a strong foundation of faith that will sustain them throughout their lives.

Church events also offer children the chance to develop important life skills, such as teamwork, leadership, and empathy. Whether they're planning a fundraiser, organizing a service project, or participating in a choir performance, children learn valuable lessons about cooperation, responsibility, and compassion. These experiences can help them grow into caring, conscientious individuals who make a positive impact on the world around them.

In conclusion, as Christian parents and adults, we have a unique opportunity to nurture our children in the ways of the Lord by encouraging them to participate in church events and activities. By doing so, we help them feel connected to their faith community, deepen their understanding of the Bible, and develop important life skills. Let us continue to support and guide our children as they grow in their faith and walk with God.

Mentorship: Relationships with church leaders and older members can offer guidance and encouragement to your children.

Mentorship is a vital aspect of raising godly children in today's world filled with temptation. It is important for Christian parents to encourage their children to foster relationships with church leaders and older members of the congregation. These individuals can offer valuable guidance and encouragement to help steer your children on the right path. By fostering these mentorship relationships, you are providing your children with a strong support system that will help them navigate the challenges of the world around them.

Church leaders play a crucial role in guiding and mentoring young members of the congregation. They can offer spiritual guidance, support, and wisdom that can help your children grow in their faith. Encouraging your children to develop relationships with church leaders can provide them with positive role models to look up to and learn from. These mentorship relationships can also help your children feel connected to their faith community and develop a sense of belonging.

Older members of the congregation also have a wealth of knowledge and experience to offer your children. Encouraging your children to seek out relationships with older members can provide them with a different perspective and valuable life lessons. These individuals can offer wisdom and guidance that comes from a lifetime of experiences, helping your children navigate the challenges they face in today's world.

By fostering mentorship relationships with church leaders and older members, you are creating a supportive network for your children to turn to when they need guidance and encouragement. These individuals can offer a listening ear, a shoulder to lean on, and words of wisdom that can help your children stay on the right path.

Encouraging your children to seek out mentorship relationships within the church community can help them grow in their faith and develop into godly individuals.

In conclusion, mentorship relationships with church leaders and older members can provide invaluable guidance and encouragement to your children as they navigate the challenges of today's world. By fostering these relationships, you are providing your children with a strong support system that will help them grow in their faith and develop into godly individuals. Encourage your children to seek out mentorship opportunities within the church community and watch as they flourish and thrive in their faith journey.

Worship and Service

In the subchapter "Worship and Service," we will explore the importance of instilling a heart of worship and a spirit of service in our children. As Christian parents and adults, we have a responsibility to nurture our children in the ways of the Lord, even in a world filled with temptation and distractions. By teaching our children to worship God and serve others, we are equipping them to navigate the challenges of life with grace and strength.

Worship is more than just attending church on Sundays. It is a lifestyle of honoring and glorifying God in all that we do. As parents, we can model a life of worship for our children by setting aside time each day for prayer, Bible reading, and singing praises to God.

Encouraging our children to develop their own personal relationship with God through prayer and worship will help them grow spiritually and draw closer to Him.

Service is another essential aspect of nurturing godly children. Jesus set the ultimate example of service by humbly washing His disciples' feet and ultimately laying down His life for us. We can teach our children the value of serving others by involving them in acts of kindness and compassion, both within our families and in the community. Whether it's volunteering at a local soup kitchen or helping a neighbor in need, service teaches our children to love and care for others as Christ did.

As we guide our children in the ways of worship and service, we are helping them develop a heart that is aligned with God's will. By nurturing a spirit of worship and service in our children, we are equipping them to make wise choices and stand firm in their faith, even in the midst of a world filled with temptation. Let us continue to encourage and sup- port our children as they grow in their relationship with God and strive to live out His love in all that they do.

In conclusion, worship and service are powerful tools that we can use to nurture godly children in an ungodly world. By teaching our children to worship God with all their hearts and serve others with love and compassion, we are laying a strong foundation for their spiritual growth and development. Let us continue to lead by example and guide our children in the ways of the Lord, knowing that our efforts will not be in vain. May we trust in God's grace and provision as we strive to raise children who are rooted in faith and equipped to shine His light in a dark world.

Regular church attendance teaches children the importance of worship and serving others. These practices become ingrained in their lives as they see them modeled by the church community.

Worship Services: Attending services together shows children the value of communal worship and reverence for God.

Attending worship services together as a family is a powerful way to instill in our children the value of communal worship and reverence for God. When we gather with other believers to praise and honor God, we are setting an example for our children to follow.

They see firsthand the importance of coming together as a community to lift up our voices in song, prayer, and praise. By consistently attending worship services as a family, we are showing our children that our faith is not just a personal matter, but something that we share with others.

As Christian parents, it is our responsibility to nurture our children in the ways of the Lord, even in a world filled with temptation and distractions. By making worship services a priority in our family's routine, we are helping to create a strong foundation of faith that will guide our children throughout their lives. Attending church together allows us to connect with other believers, receive spiritual nourishment, and grow in our relationship with God. When our children see us actively participating in worship services, they are more likely to develop a deep and lasting faith of their own.

In a world that often values individualism and self-centeredness, attending worship services as a family reminds our children that we are part of something greater than ourselves. It teaches them the importance of community, fellowship, and unity in Christ. When we come together with other believers to worship God, we are reinforcing the truth that we are all part of the body of Christ, each with a unique role to play. Our children learn that they are not alone in their faith journey, but are surrounded by a loving and supportive community of fellow believers.

Attending worship services together also provides a consistent and structured environment for our children to learn about God, His Word, and His ways. As they participate in worship, hear sermons, and engage in prayer, they are growing in their understanding of who God is and what He desires for their lives. By attending services regularly, we are helping to shape our children's spiritual development and laying a strong foundation for their faith to grow. We are providing them with the tools they need to navigate the challenges and temptations of the world with a firm grounding in God's truth.

In conclusion, attending worship services together as a family is a powerful way to nurture our children in the ways of the Lord and cultivate a deep reverence for God. By making worship a priority in our family's life, we are demonstrating the importance of communal worship, fellowship, and unity in Christ. We are providing our children with a strong foundation of faith that will guide them throughout their lives and help them navigate the challenges of an ungodly world. Let us continue to prioritize worship as a family and encourage our children to develop a deep and lasting relationship with God.

Service Projects: Involvement in service projects teaches children to live out their faith by helping those in need.

Service projects are a wonderful way to teach children about living out their faith in practical ways. By getting involved in projects that help those in need, children are able to see the importance of putting their beliefs into action. Whether it's volunteering at a soup kitchen, participating in a charity run, or simply helping out a neighbor in need, service projects provide valuable opportunities for children to learn compassion and empathy.

One of the key benefits of involvement in service projects is the sense of fulfillment and joy that it brings. When children are able to see the positive impact that their actions have on others, it can be incredibly rewarding. Not only does it help to instill a sense of pride and accomplishment, but it also fosters a sense of gratitude for the blessings that they have in their own lives. By taking part in service projects, children can learn to appreciate the value of giving back and helping those less fortunate.

Service projects also help to develop important character traits in children, such as kindness, generosity, and selfless- ness. By actively engaging in activities that benefit others, children learn to prioritize the needs of others above their own desires. This can help to cultivate a spirit of humility and empathy, as well as a sense of responsibility towards those in need. By participating in service projects, children can develop a sense of purpose

172

and a desire to make a positive difference in the world around them.

Involvement in service projects can also help children to grow in their faith and deepen their relationship with God. By putting their beliefs into action and serving others in Jesus' name, children are able to experience the love and grace of God in a tangible way. Service projects provide opportunities for children to practice the teachings of Jesus, such as loving your neighbor as yourself and caring for the least of these. Through service projects, children can learn to live out their faith in practical ways and become true Disciples of Christ.

As Christian parents and adults, it is important to encourage and support children in their involvement in service projects. By providing opportunities for children to serve others and make a difference in the world, we can help them to develop a strong foundation of faith and a deep sense of compassion. Let us continue to nurture and guide our children in their journey of faith, teaching them to live out their beliefs by helping those in need. By instilling a heart for service in our children, we are helping to shape them into Godly individuals who will make a positive impact on the world around them.

Parental Support

Parental support is crucial when it comes to raising children who are grounded in their faith and able to resist the temptations of the world. As Christian parents, it is our responsibility to provide our children with the love, guidance, and support they need to navigate the challenges they will inevitably face. By offering our unwavering support, we can help our children develop a strong foundation of faith that will carry them through the trials and temptations of life.

One of the most important ways we can support our children is by setting a positive example for them to follow. Our children look to us as role models, so it is essential that we demonstrate the values and principles we want them to embrace. By living out our faith in our daily lives, we show our children what it means to walk with God and how to resist the temptations of the world. When our children see us putting our trust in God and seeking His guidance, they are more likely to do the same.

In addition to setting a positive example, it is important to provide our children with a safe and nurturing environment where they can grow in their faith. This means creating opportunities for them to learn about God, pray, and engage in fellowship with other believers. By surrounding our children with a community of faith, we help them build relationships that will support and encourage them as they navigate the challenges of the world.

As parents, we must also be intentional about having open and honest conversations with our children about the temptations they may face. By discussing topics such as peer pressure, media influence, and societal expectations, we can help our children develop the discernment and wisdom they need to make godly choices. By being proactive in addressing these issues, we can equip our children with the tools they need to resist temptation and stay true to their faith.

Ultimately, parental support plays a vital role in nurturing godly children in an ungodly world. By setting a positive example, creating a nurturing environment, and having open conversations with our children, we can help them develop a strong foundation of faith that will guide them through life's challenges. As Christian parents, let us commit to providing our children with the love, guidance, and support they need to walk with God and resist the temptations of the world.

The church also provides support and resources for parents. Parenting classes, small groups, and pastoral counseling can offer valuable insights and encouragement.

Parenting Classes: These classes provide biblical principles and practical advice for raising children.

Parenting classes are a wonderful resource for Christian parents looking to raise their children in a way that aligns with biblical principles. These classes provide valuable insight and practical advice on how to navigate the challenges of parenting in today's world. By attending these classes, parents can gain a deeper understanding of the responsibilities and joys that come with raising children in a way that honors God.

One of the key benefits of parenting classes is the opportunity to learn from experienced instructors who can provide guidance based on biblical principles. These classes often cover a wide range of topics, including discipline, communication, and building a strong foundation of faith in the lives of our children. By participating in these classes, parents can gain valuable tools and strategies for navigating the ups and downs of parenting with grace and wisdom.

In addition to providing biblical principles, parenting classes also offer practical advice that can be applied in everyday situations. From managing behavior issues to fostering a love for God and His Word, these classes provide parents with the tools they need to raise children who are grounded in their faith and equipped to navigate the challenges of the world around them. By implementing the strategies learned in these classes, parents can create a loving and nurturing environment where their children can thrive.

Parenting classes are not just about learning new techniques or strategies; they are also an opportunity for parents to connect with other like-minded individuals who are navigating the same challenges and joys of raising godly children. By participating in these classes, parents can build a community of support and encouragement that can help them navigate the ups and downs of parenting with grace and wisdom. Together, we can learn from each other's experiences and in sights, and grow in our journey of nurturing godly children in an ungodly world.

In conclusion, parenting classes are a valuable resource for Christian parents who are looking to raise their children in a way that honors God. By learning from experienced instructors, gaining practical advice, and connecting with other parents, we can equip ourselves with the tools and support we need to navigate the challenges of parenting in today's world. Let us embrace these classes with open hearts and minds, knowing that God will guide us as we seek to nurture our children in a way that reflects His love and truth.

Support Groups: Connecting with other parents facing similar challenges can provide a sense of solidarity and shared wisdom.

Support groups can be a valuable resource for Christian parents navigating the challenges of raising godly children in an ungodly world. Connecting with other parents facing similar struggles can provide a sense of solidarity and shared wisdom. These groups offer a safe space to share experiences, seek advice, and offer encouragement to one another.

In a support group, you can find comfort in knowing that you are not alone in your journey. Other parents understand the unique challenges of raising children in today's society and can offer empathy and understanding. By connecting with like-minded individuals, you can build a community of support that will help you navigate the ups and downs of parenting with grace and strength.

In addition to emotional support, support groups can also provide practical advice and strategies for nurturing godly children. Sharing tips and resources with other parents can help you gain new insights and perspectives on parenting. By learning from each other's experiences, you can discover new approaches to discipline, communication, and spiritual guidance that can benefit your own family.

Support groups can also be a source of inspiration and motivation for Christian parents. Hearing success stories from other parents can uplift your spirits and renew your determination to raise children who are grounded in faith and values. By surrounding yourself with positive influences, you can stay focused on your goal of nurturing godly children in a world filled with temptation.

In conclusion, support groups offer a valuable opportunity for Christian parents to connect with others who share their values and beliefs. By joining a support group, you can find a sense of solidarity, shared wisdom, and encouragement that will help you navigate the challenges of parenting in today's society. Remember, you are not alone on this journey together, we can support and uplift one another as we strive to raise godly children in an ungodly world.

Prayer and Encouragement

In the journey of nurturing godly children in a world filled with temptation, prayer and encouragement are essential tools for Christian parents and adults. Prayer is our direct line of communication with God, and through it, we can seek His guidance, wisdom, and strength to navigate the challenges that come with raising children in an ungodly world. It is important to prioritize prayer in our daily lives, seeking God's will for our children and asking for His protection over them.

As Christian parents and adults, we must also provide a constant source of encouragement for our children. In a world that often seeks to tear them down and lead them astray, our words of affirmation and support can make all the differences. Let us remind our children of their worth and value in God's eyes, encouraging them to stand firm in their faith and to resist the temptations that surround them.

When we pray for our children, we are not only seeking God's intervention in their lives, but we are also setting an example for them to follow. Our children learn by example, and when they see us turning to God in times of need and relying on His strength, they are more likely to do the same. Let us lead by example, showing our children the power of prayer and the importance of seeking God's guidance in all aspects of our lives.

In moments of doubt and uncertainty, let us cling to the promises of God and find comfort in His unwavering love for us and our children. Through prayer and encouragement, we can instill in our children a strong foundation of faith that will help them navigate the challenges of this world with confidence and grace. Let us never underestimate the power of prayer and encouragement in shaping the hearts and minds of our children and guiding them towards a life filled with God's truth and love.

As we continue on this journey of nurturing godly children in an ungodly world, let us lean on God's strength and trust in His plan for our children. With prayer as our foundation and encouragement as our guide, we can raise children who are rooted in faith, equipped to resist temptation, and empowered to shine the light of God's love in a dark world. Let us never waver in our commitment to praying for and encouraging our children, knowing that God is faithful to answer our prayers and bless our efforts to raise godly children in a world of temptation.

The church community can be a source of prayer and encouragement for your family. Knowing that others are praying for your children's growth and wellbeing is a tremendous support.

Prayer Groups: Joining a prayer group allows you to share your concerns and receive prayer support.

Prayer Groups: Joining a prayer group allows you to share your concerns and receive prayer support. As Christian parents and adults, we understand the importance of surrounding ourselves with like-minded individuals who can provide encouragement and support in our faith journey. Prayer groups offer a unique opportunity to come together in fellowship and lift each other up in prayer.

When you join a prayer group, you are not only opening yourself up to receiving prayer support, but you are also committing to being a source of strength and encouragement for others. By sharing your concerns and burdens with your fellow group members, you are allowing them to come alongside you and intercede on your behalf. This sense of community and support can be a powerful tool in navigating the challenges of raising godly children in a world filled with temptation.

Prayer groups provide a safe space for you to be vulnerable and transparent about your struggles and triumphs. In this environment, you can share your joys and sorrows, knowing that you are surrounded by individuals who are committed to praying for you and offering words of encouragement. This sense of unity and camaraderie can be a source of comfort and strength as you seek to nurture your children in a world that often goes against the values and teachings of our faith.

Joining a prayer group also allows you to deepen your relationship with God through regular prayer and reflection. As you come together with others to pray, you are creating a space for God to move in your life and the lives of those around you. By setting aside time to seek God's guidance and wisdom in a communal setting, you are opening yourself up to experiencing His presence in a tangible way.

In conclusion, joining a prayer group is a valuable opportunity for Christian parents and adults to come together in fellowship, share their concerns, and receive prayer support. By surrounding yourself with a community of believers who are committed to lifting each other up in prayer, you can find strength, encouragement, and guidance as you seek to nurture godly children in a world of temptation. Let us embrace the power of prayer groups and the blessings that come from joining together in faith.

Encouragement: Fellow believers can offer words of encouragement and affirmations, helping you stay strong in your parenting journey.

As Christian parents, we face many challenges in today's world as we strive to raise our children in a way that honors God. It can often feel like an uphill battle, especially when we see the temptations and pressures that our children are exposed to on a daily basis. In times like these, it is important to remember that we are not alone in our parenting journey.

Fellow believers can offer words of encouragement and affirmation, helping us stay strong in our faith and in our commitment to nurturing godly children.

When we surround ourselves with other Christian parents, we are able to draw strength from their experiences and wisdom. They can offer us words of encouragement when we are feeling discouraged or overwhelmed, reminding us that we are not alone in our struggles. Their support can help us stay focused on our goal of raising children who love and serve the Lord, even in the face of worldly temptations.

It is important to seek out fellow believers who can offer us this kind of encouragement. This may be through a church small group, a parenting support group, or even just a close group of friends who share our faith. By building these relationships, we create a community of support that can help us navigate the challenges of parenting in today's world.

In turn, we can also offer words of encouragement and affirmation to our fellow Christian parents. By sharing our own experiences and offering a listening ear, we can help lift up others who may be struggling in their parenting journey. We can remind them of the importance of staying strong in their faith and staying committed to raising godly children, even when the world around us may seem to be pulling us in the opposite direction.

Ultimately, by coming together as a community of believers, we can find strength and encouragement to continue on our journey of nurturing godly children in an ungodly world. Let us remember that we are not alone in this task, and let us lean on each other for support and guidance as we strive to raise children who love and honor the Lord.

By actively involving your family in church life, you provide your children with additional resources and support to strengthen their faith. The church complements your efforts at home, creating a well-rounded environment for your children's spiritual growth.

As Christian parents, we are constantly seeking ways to nurture and strengthen our children's faith in a world filled with temptation. One powerful way to do this is by actively involving our families in church life. By participating in church activities, attending services together, and engaging in community outreach programs, we can provide our children with additional resources and support to help them grow in their relationship with God.

The church serves as a complement to our efforts at home, creating a well-rounded environment for our children's spiritual growth. While we can instill values and beliefs in our children within the walls of our own home, the church offers a broader community of support and encouragement. Through interactions with other believers, participation in youth groups and Sunday school classes, and exposure to different perspectives within the faith, our children can deep- en their understanding of God and His love for them.

When we involve our families in church life, we are not only strengthening our children's faith, but we are also building a strong foundation for their future. By prioritizing regular attendance at church services and events, we are teaching our children the importance of worship, fellowship, and service to others. These values will stay with them as they navigate the challenges of the world and make decisions that align with their faith.

Furthermore, by actively involving our families in church life, we are setting an example for our children to follow. When they see us participating in church activities, volunteering our time, and engaging in meaningful conversations about our faith, they are more likely to do the same. Our actions speak louder than words, and by showing our children the importance of incorporating faith into every aspect of our lives, we are guiding them on a path toward spiritual growth and maturity.

In conclusion, by actively involving our families in church life, we are providing our children with the resources and support they need to strengthen their faith. The church complements our efforts at home, creating a well-rounded environment for our children's spiritual growth. As Christian parents, let us continue to prioritize our family's involvement in church activities, knowing that we are laying a solid foundation for our children's future and helping them navigate the challenges of the world with a strong and unwavering faith in God.

With the church's partnership, you can confidently raise godly children, knowing they are surrounded by a loving and supportive faith community.

As Christian parents, we understand the weight of responsibility that comes with raising children in today's world. It can be challenging to navigate through the temptations and dis- tractions that seem to be lurking around every corner. However, we want to remind you that you are not alone in this journey. With the church's partnership, you can confidently raise godly children, knowing they are surrounded by a loving and supportive faith community.

The church plays a vital role in nurturing and guiding our children in their faith journey. By actively participating in church activities, children are given the opportunity to grow in their relationship with God and develop a strong foundation of faith. Through Sunday school, youth groups, and other programs, our children can learn about the teachings of Jesus and the importance of living a life that reflects His love and grace.

It is comforting to know that our children are not only learning about God within the walls of our home but also within the supportive environment of the church. This partnership allows us as parents to rest assured that our children are being surrounded by positive influences and role models who are dedicated to helping them grow in their faith. The church provides a sense of community and belonging that is essential for our children to thrive spiritually.

By actively involving our children in church activities, we are instilling in them a sense of belonging to a larger family of believers. This sense of community helps our children feel supported and loved, knowing that they have a network of people who are there to encourage and guide them along their spiritual journey. The church's partnership serves as a valuable resource for us as parents as we seek to raise our children in a way that honors God and reflects His love for others.

In conclusion, we want to encourage you, as Christian parents, to embrace the partnership with the church in raising godly children. By actively involving your children in church activities and programs, you are providing them with a strong foundation of faith and supportive communities that will help them navigate through the challenges of the world. With the church's partnership, you can confidently raise your children, knowing that they are surrounded by a loving and supportive faith community that is dedicated to helping them grow in their relationship with God.

ABOUT THE AUTHOR

Romoking Onyebum is a dedicated pastor and accomplished entrepreneur with a diverse portfolio of successful businesses. He is the founder of Abroad Investment Limited, a company known for its innovative approach to investment opportunities. In addition to his entrepreneurial endeavors, Romoking is a skilled cloud engineer and a seasoned realtor, bringing a wealth of expertise and experience to each of his ventures.

His passion for both faith and business uniquely positions him to guide and inspire others in their personal and professional journeys.

www.ingramcontent.com/pod-product-compliance
Lightning Source LLC
LaVergne TN
LVHW020055090426
835513LV00029B/1536